The Magic of Skye

By the same author,
uniform with this volume:

The Welsh Peaks
The Scottish Peaks
The Peak and Pennines
The Lakeland Peaks

Plate 1 Marsco and Glen Sligachan

W. A. Poucher Hon F.R.P.S.

The Magic of Skye

With 152 photographs by the author

Constable London

First published in Great Britain 1949
by Chapman and Hall Ltd

Second edition published 1980
by Constable and Company Ltd
3 The Lanchesters, 162 Fulham Palace Road,
London W6 9ER

Reprinted 1982, 1986, 1991, 1996

Third edition published 1989

Set in Monophoto Times New Roman 9pt
Filmset and printed in Great Britain by
BAS Printers Limited, Over Wallop, Hampshire

To The Good Companions

After Mr Poucher's death in August 1988, at the age of 96, his son and daughter-in-law felt that as he had loved the Island so much, it would be appropriate for there to be some form of memorial to him on Skye. So with the agreement of Mr Ian S. Campbell, a memorial seat was presented to the Sligachan Hotel, where it was placed in the garden. The plaque reads:

IN MEMORY OF
WALTER POUCHER 1891–1988
A RENOWNED MOUNTAIN PHOTOGRAPHER
WHO LOVED THE WILD PLACES

There are many who have seen one or other aspect of the wonderful beauty of Skye, but owing to the shortness of holidays and to the vagaries of the weather, there are few who have had either time or opportunity to discover much of the strange loveliness of this marvellous isle.

The motorist has travelled there and viewed these enchanting scenes from his car; the pedestrian has visited them also and perhaps been spellbound by the grotesque rock architecture of the Storr and Quiraing; the angler has gone there too and in solitude plied his rod and line by lonely loch or bubbling burn in the very shadow of these places; whilst the mountaineer has returned there again and again to scale the fantastic peaks of the Coolins and to feast his eyes on the superb panorama revealed only to those who can reach the lofty viewpoint.

I went to the Misty Isle in the spring, determined to brave the elements, to face the risks of the solitary climber, and to wait patiently for those elusive conditions of atmosphere and lighting which impart an intangible mystery to this dramatic landscape; all in an effort to capture the Magic of Skye with my camera.

The pages of this book unfold the tale of this journey and may transport the reader to many places which are perhaps inaccessible to him and beyond the powers of attainment to others. They will doubtless excite the imagination of those who know this wild country, and they may be a revelation to others who are unfamiliar with it, but if they induce them to go there and see for themselves, then it will be a compliment to this island, the brightest jewel of our homeland.

W. A. POUCHER

This book was first published thirty years ago at the price of thirty shillings and when all copies had been sold a new edition was clearly impossible owing to the phenomenal increase in gravure printing costs. In the intervening period the price asked by owners of the book who were prepared to sell rose so high in the past decade that copies in immaculate condition changed hands for around £50, while even those in poor condition fetched half this price. For, according to reviewers, *The Magic of Skye* was the classic work on the Misty Isle and had now become a collector's piece.

I received hundreds of letters requesting a new edition and it was only in the spring of last year, while I was in Glen Brittle Campsite, that many climbers asked why the book could not be published in the smaller format of my four Pictorial Guides. When I suggested this to my present publishers they agreed, so here it is with my best wishes to all climbers and scramblers and with the hope that the smaller plates will enjoy their former appeal.

There are eight new photographs. Some of them are replacements and the others illustrate the new monograph on Waterstein Head, which I felt would complete the coverage of the island.

There is no change in the text excepting the heights of the Peaks and Bealachs, which were communicated to me by the Ordnance Survey after they had fixed the correct altitudes by Stereo-comparator.

I have deleted the Photographic Data because the early Leica cameras I used are no longer available.

W. A. POUCHER
4 Heathfield
Reigate Heath, Surrey

As my late father wrote in 1980 in his preface to the second edition, that edition was being published some thirty years after the book originally appeared. Since then *The Magic of Skye* has been reprinted twice, and now, another ten years on, the publishers have asked me to suggest any changes I felt necessary to bring it up to date once more.

I have found little in the text that required alteration and have merely amended an item or two about roads in the section on accessibility and updated the location of youth hostels on the island.

However, as the original index was not considered sufficiently comprehensive by some readers, I have completely re-done this and added a separate index of photographic plates for their convenience.

I feel that this work, together with my late father's *Skye*, contains a collection of black and white and colour photographs which will both bring back happy memories to those who already know this beautiful island and show those who are visiting it for the first time what delights they may expect.

JOHN POUCHER
Gate Ghyll, High Brigham
Cockermouth, Cumbria

Contents

Skye is the largest of the many beautiful islands lying off the west coast of Scotland and is part of Inverness-shire. It has an area of approximately 350,000 acres (approx 150,000 hectares), is fifty miles (84·5 km) long from north to south, and from seven (11·83 km) to twenty-five (42·25 km) broad. Every part of it is isolated from another by bens, glens, burns and winding sea lochs; the latter being responsible for its extensive coastline which measures hundreds of miles and is out of all proportion to its small area. No point on the island is more than five miles (8·45 km) from the sea.

The Isle of Skye is characterised by numerous peninsulas and if its central focus is taken as west of Sligachan, they all appear to fly outwards and suggest some strange species of wild-fowl. A glance at the map will confirm this peculiarity which may account for its early name of the Winged Isle—Eilean Sgiathanach from the Gaelic *Sgiath*, a wing. To Ossian, however, and to many modern writers also, it is known always as Eilean a Cheo, the Isle of Mist. A closer study of the map will reveal the prominence of the northern and southern peninsulas, whereas to the east and west they appear to be considerably shortened and deeply indented by narrow sea lochs. Moreover, they afford an infinite variety of terrain and coastline, a fact which is immediately apparent to the traveller who is bent upon a detailed exploration of the island.

The northern peninsulas are noteworthy for their wild and desolate moorland, rising to no inconsiderable height, and in Trotternish dominated by the most bizarre collection of rocks in Britain. Here a continuous ridge forms a great backbone with shattered precipitous cliffs facing the east and gently swelling slopes falling to the west. The Quiraing and Leac na' Fionn occupy an unrivalled position at its northern tip opposite Flodigarry and reveal on the one side the gleaming hills of the Outer Hebrides, and on the other the dim outline of the mountain ranges of the Northern Counties. The Storr, with its conspicuous Old Man, rises to nearly 3,000 feet (914 m) at its southern end and assumes an importance in the landscape which has to be seen to be believed, for it appears on the horizon from a variety of widely separated and distant viewpoints. Vaternish and Duirinish lie to the west but their uplands are lacking in such outstanding geographical features. They nevertheless mount to considerable altitudes, are generally rounded, but in the case of Macleod's Tables have prominent flattened tops whose heathery flanks sink down gradually to the sea. In the south the region takes on the character of upland country again, but with a notable difference, for the northern desolation is replaced by a fertility and richness of aspect which has given it the name of the 'Garden of Skye'.

The great mountain range straddles the island at its centre and presents a strange contrast by its two distinct types of topography. The Red Hills are huddled together to the north-east; they are bulky rounded cones and pyramids, with long streaks of scree to relieve their monotony. The Black Coolins rise to the south-west as a magnificent twisting ridge whose flanks are steep and precipitous, and whose crest is adorned by a succession of jagged, spiry peaks which are the most spectacular in the whole of Britain. They completely dominate the Skye landscape and are the delight of the mountaineer. Blaven stands to the south-east of them in splendid isolation and is considered by many to be the most beautiful mountain in the country.

All this vast solitude, save the barren gabbro of the Coolins and the naked granite of the Red Hills, is covered with heather, bent and bracken, while the lower slopes of the moorland disclose the nodding white heads of the cotton grass, and on the warm summer days the bog myrtle exhales a fragrance that impregnates the breeze for an incredible distance. Sheep wander at will over much of the billowy moors, and crofters find a peaceful livelihood on the more fertile stretches near the sea. Here solitude has not to be searched for; it can be found within a short distance of any habitation. You may meander by tinkling burns in green valleys, stride across miles of desolate brown peat hags, or ascend the gentler slopes of the bens for days on end without meeting another living soul and all the time your horizon will be the hills or the sea.

These are some of the inimitable charms of Skye, but they are not all, for the island seaboard is one of its most dramatic features and presents much of the finest coast scenery in the country. Here great basaltic cliffs hang their castellated fronts a thousand feet above the sundering tides of the ocean, windy headlands in plenty display lofty cliff formations whose sea edges are often riddled with caves, while some of the bays have such graceful sweeping curves that their beauty is for ever imprinted on the memory of the bewildered, but enchanted, wayfarer.

Accessibility

Those who know Skye will agree that I have not painted this brief picture of the island in too glowing colours, and those who have yet to make its acquaintance but have merely scanned the pictures in this book, will be prepared to admit that its wonderful scenery is on a higher plane than much of our island heritage. They will doubtless make up their minds to go there and see it for themselves at the first opportunity, but they may be deterred by its apparent remoteness, not so much from the towns of Scotland, but more particularly from the cities of southern England and Wales. Modern travel, however, has reduced such journeys to a minimum of discomfort and those who decide to go by rail have a choice between the routes from Euston to the Kyle of Lochalsh *via* Inverness and that from King's Cross to Mallaig by way of Glasgow and Fort William. Although the former is more circuitous there is not much difference in the time needed— well under 24 hours—to reach such destinations as Sligachan or Portree. But if the traveller is anxious to select the most picturesque route then he will choose the latter because the railway from Glasgow goes through some fine country to Fort William and thereafter threads one of the loveliest succession of glens in the whole of Scotland, known familiarly as the 'Road to the Isles'. There is also a further attraction in this approach, for the steamer may be taken as far as Portree, instead of stepping off it at Armadale, and this enables the visitor to sail through the Sound of Sleat, past the islands of Pabay, Scalpay and Raasay, before finally entering the land-locked harbour of the 'Metropolis' of Skye. The panorama throughout is of the highest order and forms a fitting prelude to the discovery of the charms of the island itself.

For those who prefer to travel inland in Skye by road, for there are no railways, there are excellent bus services connecting with all the ferries. The sea crossing from the Kyle of Lochalsh to Kyleakin is under half a mile, while that from Mallaig to Armadale is only just over five miles. The buses run to such remote places as Flodigarry by way of Portree, and to Dunvegan *via* Sligachan. The distances between the places of interest are not great but they are nevertheless considerable, and while taxis are available for those who are prepared to pay for them, the use of one's own car has decided advantages. It is well over 600 miles (1,014 km) from London to Portree but I have completed the journey comfortably in two days from my Surrey home. The road through the Western Highlands by way of Loch Lomond, Fort William and Dornie is enchanting, and as the latter place now has a bridge instead of a ferry, there is no irritating delay such as there used to be. The main roads on Skye are good, particularly that from Kyleakin to Uig, which was considerably improved to cater for the ferry traffic to the Outer Isles. The subsidiary roads, though narrower, are normally kept in good repair.

There is, at present, no scheduled air service to Skye.

Accommodation

Accommodation in Skye is moderately good but by no means on a sufficiently adequate scale to meet the demands. Some of the hotels are very well run, with comfortable beds and excellent food to say nothing of the well stocked wine cellars, while others offer the usual amenities without being ostentatious. There are Youth Hostels at Armadale, Broadford, Glen Brittle, Kyleakin, Uig and on Raasay and most of the towns and villages have rooms which can be booked in advance. The best centres for the motorist are Sligachan and Portree because roads radiate to all parts of the island from these places. Glen Brittle and Sligachan are the only centres for the mountaineer, the former for the greater part of the main Coolins Ridge, the latter for its northern section ending at Sgurr nan Gillean. The road between these two centres is fifteen miles (25·35 km) long and the burns which were at one time crossed by water splashes are now bridged. A pleasant track for walkers over the Bealach a' Mhaim joins them and is eight miles (13.52 km) long. Blaven is so far away from both places that climbers would be well advised to stay either in Broadford or Elgol; if in the former they will have to motor to the latter or to Kirkibost for the commencement of the ascent. Those who wish to explore Quiraing and Leac na 'Fionn should stay at Flodigarry which is only two miles (3·38 km) away and delightfully situated on high ground overlooking Staffin Bay. It affords an unequalled prospect of the long line of peaks on the mainland from Suilven to Ben Sgriol, and moreover, as Duntulm is but four miles (6·75 km) away on the other side of Trotternish, it allows ample time in which to visit this relic of the past glories of the Macdonalds.

Weather

The Western Highlands have a reputation for bad weather and conditions in the Misty Isle are often said to be even worse, but if I am to judge it by my own experiences, then I contend that both claims are exaggerated, provided the visitor goes there at the right time of the year. It is, however, true enough that Skye lies right in the path of the prevailing south-westerly winds and that the warm moisture-laden air from the Atlantic condenses on being blown against the cold hillsides with eventual precipitation as rain. This is, of course, characteristic of all the ranges of hills on the western seaboard of Britain, and from my long experiences of them all, Skye and the Western Highlands are no wetter places than either English Lakeland or Snowdonia. Much depends upon the time of year the traveller is able to visit these districts and as a rule the best chances of sunny conditions are from May to the middle of July. The more usual holiday months are August and September, and while this season possibly yields the most lovely colouring because the heather is then in bloom, it is a notoriously bad time for rain and haze both of which detract considerably from full enjoyment. North-westerly winds bring the finest pageants of the sky and visibility is then occasionally so phenomenal that the islands of Rhum and Canna, to say nothing of those away across the Minch, appear to lie unbelieveably close to the shore. Most wayfarers carry a camera on their holidays and it is at such times that they revel in the magical lighting, the amazing scenery, and the glory of the cloud-flecked skies.

Maps and compass

Maps are just as important in Skye as elsewhere and if the visitor intends to climb in the Coolins they are absolutely indispensable. The best sheet for general use is the half-inch Special District Relief Map issued by the Ordnance Survey: it is contoured on the layer system, includes the whole of the island as well as Rhum and Canna, and brings in the mainland as far east as Dornie. A mere glance at it affords a true conception of the undulations of the country and is not confused by the introduction of too many colours. The one-inch (and 1 : 50,000) O.S. sheets contain more detail, as would be expected, but unhappily they are on four sheets, two of which cut right across the Coolins. A useful addition is the quarter-inch map which includes the Outer Islands in their entirety and a long strip of the mainland from Scourie in the north to Loch Eil in the south. This facilitates the identification of their numerous peaks which are seen from almost every viewpoint on the island. The excellent Relief Map of the whole of Skye was issued in 1932 and is no longer available. Hence, the best replacement at present is Bartholomew's 1 : 100,000 Skye and Torridon No. 54, and for the Coolins O.S. 1 : 25,000 Leisure Map, which is backed by the Torridon Hills.

Those who intend to traverse the main ridge of the Coolins, to climb its splintered peaks, or to cross its passes, should be in possession of the Special Map issued by the Scottish Mountaineering Club. It is on a scale of four inches to the mile and is reproduced from the six-inch Ordnance Survey map of Scotland. While the contouring system is scarcely as clear as one might wish, it is nevertheless the best map of these hills available and its usefulness is enhanced by the inclusion of red lines which indicate the many walking routes, and of dotted lines which differentiate them from those where scrambling is necessary. Another map of the Coolins included in this Club's early Guide to the Island was on a scale of three inches to the mile (7·62 cm to 1·69 km) and specially contoured to give greater clarity to the main features of the Coolins ridge, but it is missing from the present series.

Mountaineers always make a point of carrying a compass on their expeditions, but since much of the Coolins is built of magnetic rock, the compass needle just spins round and the instrument is useless. Bearing this in mind, all climbers who are not familiar with this magnificent group of hills should not venture on them for the first time on misty days, if they wish to keep out of trouble. The best plan is to note their topography on the clear days so that when the mist suddenly comes down, or rises, which is quite a common occurrence, they do not hesitate as to which side of the ridge to descend. If perchance they go down the wrong side and are able to reach the low ground in safety, they will probably find themselves on the shore of Loch Coruisk with a twenty mile (33·8 km) walk back to their hotel.

Geology

Those who have read my *Highland Holiday* will remember that I mentioned therein the strange geology of Arran; the smooth barren glens, the enormous dykes, and the astonishing Cyclopean walls of granite, all of which help to make the wonderful mountain landscape of that enchanting isle.

The geology of Skye is no less fascinating. The whole island is built upon a series of sedimentary rocks: gneissose and schistose, and dark red sandstone occurring in Sleat; varieties of the Jurassic series, full of fossils, in Strathaird, and at the base of the long line of cliffs stretching northwards from Sligachan to the tip of Trotternish. The great volcanic series were laid down above them in the Tertiary age and thus form the youngest ranges of mountains in the whole of Britain.

The earlier series of rocks have not contributed materially to the weird scenery of Skye, but a few of them are nevertheless worthy of mention. For instance, the earliest are pre-Cambrian and form the peninsula of Sleat, while the Cambrian series is represented at Ord and in the district of Strath. Jurassic beds occur on the east coast of Trotternish and are capped by Tertiary basalts which rise far above sea level. They may be found also on the shores of Loch Slapin and in the vicinity of Broadford. The Middle Lias formation is well represented at Prince Charlie's Cave and in the cliffs of Ben Tianavaig, south of Portree Bay and facing Raasay. The Lower Oolite group occurs here also and in the Strathaird district is found immediately below the sheets of basalt. The Great Estuarine series appear at Aird, Duntulm and inland round the Storr lochs, whilst the last member of the Jurassic system, the Oxford Clay series, occurs at great elevations on the east coast but dips away towards the west below the level of the sea. It formed a very insecure foundation for the great cap of basalt which accounts for the shattered masses of Storr and Quiraing.

The Volcanic series of rocks formed during the Tertiary period are responsible for the striking beauty of Skye and are divided roughly into three classes: (1) the plateaux basalts; (2) gabbro; (3) granophyre rocks. They have been altered and modified throughout the ages by denudation, by the erosive action of water, and finally by ice, but they still preserve their characteristic forms as may be observed on the terraced tablelands of Trotternish, the angular, jagged and spiry peaks of the Coolins, and the smooth rounded Red Hills respectively.

Volcanic activity ceased over the British Isles after the last outbreak of Permian time and the Mesozonic period passed without its revival. It was, however, resumed on a gigantic scale with the dawn of the Tertiary epoch, but with many intervals of quiescence, as has been proved by the discovery of sedimentary materials and even animal and plant remains between the successive sheets of plateaux basalts. The gabbro of the Coolins indicates a new period of activity, when enormous masses of molten rock were upheaved and intruded among the sheets of basalt. The Red Hills on the other hand resulted from a subterranean outflow which never reached the surface.

The Sills are also a prominent feature in Skye and are due to sheets of molten lava being injected between the planes of other rock, such as sheets of basalt, or between them and the Jurassic strata below. The Dykes are also of volcanic origin when the lava broke through not only the basalts, but also the gabbros and the granophyres of both Coolins and Red Hills. When composed of harder material than their surroundings they project as wall-like masses of crystallised lava, but when of softer constitution they have decayed and left a fissure opening between walls of more solid rock.

Mountaineers who have climbed in the Coolins will have been fascinated by the strange and unique rock formations they have encountered. Some detailed geological notes about them may, therefore, be of interest, and I have taken as my authority the works of Dr. Alfred Harker and Sir Archibald Geikie, two eminent geologists who have studied this terrain. A reference to the numerous photographs in this volume will amply illustrate the many examples cited.

The Coolins contain the largest area of gabbro in Britain and the range includes Blaven which is separated from the main chain by Glen Sligachan. Newcomers to the district will at once notice that the rock provides holds for hands and feet of such exceptional security that they are able to climb faces of sensational steepness with comparative ease. Although it is hard and tough, this peculiar quality is due to the unequal weathering of its component minerals which results in an extreme roughness of surface that soon wears the skin off the climber's finger tips!

As I have said, considerable patches of basalt have been intruded into this vast area of gabbro, and owing to its more brittle nature, it affords insecure holds. Examples well known to the climber are the cone of Sgurr Alasdair, together with the peaks of Thearlaich and Mhic Coinnich, while the scrambler will have encountered it on Gars-bheinn and on the ridge running up to Bruach na Frithe from the Bealach a 'Mhaim.

The lie of the strata will have been apparent to all those who have traversed the main Coolins ridge. This is due to the intrusion in the gabbro of the plateaux basalts already referred to and also to the presence of Dolorite. It will also have been noticed that these great sheets of rock have an inclined plane of no dissimilar angle and that they all lean towards the centre of the range. For instance, the tilt of Sgurr na Stri is to the north and of Sgurr nan Gillean to the south. The gigantic slabs of Ghreadaidh, Banachdich, Dearg and nan Eag are, however, more conspicuous in their fall to the east, and those of Clach Glas less so in their inclination to the west. In some of these examples the crest of the ridge is formed by the edge of the uppermost sheet, as in Dearg and nan Eag, but in both cases it will be remembered how the opposing flanks are in marked contrast: on the east relatively smooth and on the west much shattered; a feature often taken advantage of by climbers who traverse the ledges on the outside. The great bend in the main ridge at Sgurr a 'Mhadaidh provides a striking example of this trend and is especially noticeable when seen from the south-west peak of the group. Here the sheets of rock lie across the ridge which in consequence is much broken and forms a succession of summits.

The Basalt and Dolorite Dykes which have decayed more rapidly than the adjacent gabbro have resulted in prominent fissures in the group and are well seen in the Pinnacle Ridge of Sgurr nan Gillean, where they run at right angles, and in the Waterpipe Gully of Sgurr an Fheadain and the gullies of Blaven and Bidein Druim nan Ramh where they tilt with the slopes of the peaks themselves. In several instances they have, on the contrary, withstood the weathering and are noticeable as projections and isolated walls such as those which abound near the Alasdair-Sgumain col, and of course the conspicuous Inaccessible Pinnacle on Sgurr Dearg which is composed of Trap rock.

During the Great Ice Age the Coolins were probably submerged, and, although the glaciers played their part in the formation of the valleys as is apparent around Loch Coruisk, running water may have had a greater influence upon the final topography of the group. Glacial erosion is, however, responsible for the amphitheatre form of the corries and also for their steep faces. This is also a noticeable feature of the dividing line between Lota and Harta Corries, and for the precipitous drops in Corries Lagan and Ghrunnda.

The Coolins consist of two well defined groups of hills separated by Glen Sligachan and Strath na Creitheach, the valley extending for a long eight miles (13·52 km), from the Sligachan Hotel southwards to Camasunary on the shores of Loch Scavaig. The Red Hills are huddled together in the north-east corner of the range with the symmetrical cone of Glamaig at one end and the superbly proportioned Marsco at the other. They are connected by an elevated ridge which undulates over the three tops of Beinn Dearg. The Blaven group lies to the south and is dominated by this glorious mountain which affords a beautiful skyline from all the peaks of the main Coolins ridge on the other side of Glen Sligachan. It is joined to its northern satellite of Gharbh-bheinn by the fantastic pinnacled ridge of Clach Glas, and thereafter tails away northwards in the direction of Loch Ainort, passing over Belig to end at Glas Bheinn Mhor. Whilst the majestic elevation of this group excites the admiration of all who view it from the west, it is just as lovely when seen from Torrin and Loch Slapin on the east.

The Main Ridge of the Black Coolins commences in the south with the beautiful cone of Gars-bheinn which frowns in splendid isolation upon the vast expanse of Loch Scavaig. It follows a twisting course northwards and at Bruach na Frithe turns sharply to the east as far as Sgurr nan Gillean, to bend south again and terminate with the striking wedge-shaped peak of Sgurr na h 'Uamha. The chain is continuous: the narrow lofty ridge linking the numerous individual summits in pendant sweeps which rarely fall much below the 3,000 feet (914 m) contour, excepting at one or two of the Bealachs, and at the great gash between Sgurr na Bhairnich and An Caisteal. Sgurr Alasdair is the highest peak and rises towards the southern end of the chain, while Sgurr nah 'Uamha is the lowest and situated at its northern extremity. Sgurr nan Gillean has the most graceful lines from almost any angle but from the south-east assumes the proportions of a stately cathedral spire.

Lateral ridges support the main chain and are confusing in

mist to those climbers who are not familiar with the topography of their junctions. They enclose numerous wild corries which vary from the gigantic savage depression cupping Loch Coruisk, to the green flower-decked hollow of Fionn Choire. The latter is the exception rather than the rule because the vast scree slopes of disintegrated gabbro provide a poor soil for vegetation. The Bealachs usually occur as narrow door-like cracks in the main ridge and afford a passage from the inner corries of the group to those outside. They are sometimes of striking proportions with sheer walls of rock soaring skywards and those who pass over them in either direction are generally arrested by the dramatic change of scene which is suddenly disclosed on the clear days.

All this grandeur is only revealed to the seasoned ridge wanderer who may walk, scramble and rock climb to his heart's content from one end of the Coolins to the other. Whilst the ridge itself provides every aspect of mountaineering interest, save perhaps that of a glacier traverse, there is a spacious panorama in all directions which includes the sea and the dim outline of the Outer Islands, as well as hosts of the mainland peaks.

Seen from the lower levels of the glens, from the peninsulas of the west, or even from the sea itself, the Coolins assume an individuality and magnificence which immediately places them in a class by themselves. When measured in mere altitude they are inferior to many of the mountains on the mainland of Scotland and to several of the peaks in North Wales, but it is their subtle colouring, their strange pageantry of rain and mist, sunshine and cloud, their splendid elevation on the edge of the restless ocean, and the mountain mystery enfolding them—a secret beauty born of their atmosphere and lighting—which endear them to all who return again and again to pay homage.

Skye without the Coolins would be like a play without its hero. It is Nature's masterpiece of the Hebrides.

Easy ways for the walker
As I have already pointed out, there are only two centres for those who wish to explore the Coolins—Glen Brittle for its southern section, and Sligachan for the northern end of the range

and for the Red Hills. Lock Coruisk is roughly equidistant
from them both, but it is possible to sail from Glen Brittle to the
head of Loch Scavaig and thus avoid the long walk around the
steep flanks of Gars-bheinn. Blaven is best climbed from the
Strathaird district, although its traverse together with that of
Clach Glas may be accomplished in a long day from Sligachan,
the approach being shortened by taking the early morning bus to
the head of Loch Ainort.

At first sight tourists with no mountaineering experience may
imagine these hills to be utterly inaccessible. This, however, is not
the case, and in order to facilitate the choice of routes I shall
briefly indicate them here although in several instances I have
described and illustrated them fully in the sections which follow.

GLEN SLIGACHAN. This should be the first walk undertaken by
the initiate because the glen deeply penetrates the fastnesses of
the group. Although the going is rough but easy, the stern
ruggedness of the mountains is gradually unfolded and this closer
contact with them will act as a deterrent for any rash expedition
that might have been contemplated after viewing them only from
afar. Some pedestrians may get no further than the Dubh Lochs,
but strong walkers will reach Camasunary. It is never advisable
to hurry amid such grand scenery, and each of the changing
aspects of the hills should be examined and their topography
carefully noted. That part of the walk along the flank of Blaven
will doubtless create a lasting impression of the splendour and
vastness of its precipitous western face.

LOCH CORUISK. In the walk down Glen Sligachan a cairn will
be noticed just to the south of the Dubh Lochs where the track
forks. The left branch leads to Camasunary and the right one to
Loch Coruisk. The path breasting the shoulder of the Druim
Hain ridge is clearly seen ahead, and on attaining the large cairn
on its crest, Loch Coruisk is observed below and beyond the
lochan on the far side of the ridge.

SGURR NA STRI. I consider this to be the best viewpoint in the
whole district. It stands at the head of Loch Scavaig immediately
opposite Gars-bheinn and is about halfway between this
mountain and Blaven. Its superiority as a coign of vantage is due

not only to its position, but also to its height: the former allows
of a full length prospect of Loch Coruisk and of Coir-uisg at its
head, together with an unrivalled panorama of the whole Coolins
ridge which appears as a vast amphitheatre enclosing them; the
latter is ideal because it only rises to 1,631 feet (497 m) and thus
enables the observer to appreciate correctly the scale of this long
chain of peaks. Sgurr na Stri is easily approached from the cairn
on the Druim Hain ridge by walking southwards along its
shattered crest until the western top is attained. It is an
expedition for strong walkers only as the distance there and back
to Sligachan is not much less than twenty miles (33·8 km).

HARTA CORRIE. This wild recess is entered from Glen
Sligachan, the Bloody Stone being passed on the left. Although
there is an indistinct track on the west bank of the Sligachan
River, it is easier to follow that on the east bank as far as the
Dubh Lochs, and then to cross the glen between them. This
corrie of solitudes and weird desolation might well have been one
of Nature's primeval workshops: its effect is overpowering.

MARSCO. This well-placed and magnificently proportioned
mountain will have excited the admiration of all those lovers of
the hills who have stood on the bridge over the Sligachan River
and, in the soft light of evening, gazed down the glen when the
pink-tinted clouds have rolled off Sgurr nan Gillean to be
dissipated above Blaven. It is an easy afternoon climb by way of
its northern slopes leading to the ridge on the west side of Coire
nan Laogh. The cairn affords striking views of the surrounding
hills and especially of Sgurr nan Gillean on the opposite side of
the glen.

GLAMAIG. This is the sentinel which frowns eternally upon the
Sligachan Inn, and most of the people who stay there, climb it
from the loch side and make the circuit of the Beinn Dearg tops
on the way back to the hotel. Its mossy summit reveals an
extensive panorama, across the inland seas, backed by the dim
hills of the mainland. The steep angle of the slopes of Glamaig,
coupled with its screes, make the ascent a hard one, but there are
no risks whatever and the views are rewarding.

THE SLIGACHAN LOCHANS. Those who like to wander over the

moors and peat hags will find much to interest them within a stone's throw of the Inn. Loch Mor na Caiplaich lies on the high ground between the Portree and Dunvegan roads, and Loch an Eilean is just off the latter about a mile away. When in spate, the burns coming down from the Coolins are worth a visit. They display some lovely cataracts and waterfalls, often enclosed by wild ravines. Those of the two Red Burns are especially fascinating.

BRUACH NA FRITHE. This is the one Coolins peak that may be reached by an easy walk. Follow the Red Burn to within half a mile of the Bealach a 'Mhaim, then cross it and follow one of its tributaries coming down from Fionn Choire. When it peters out on the high ground, pick up the cairned track which rises in the bed of the corrie and ultimately leads over the scree to the ridge near the Bealach nan Lice. Turn to the right along its crest and walk up to the cairn on Bruach na Frithe which reveals the complete S bend of the main ridge to the south. This scene is best observed in the late afternoon when the sun is in the west, for the lighting then clearly delineates its salient features. The first bend to the left ends at Sgurr na Bhairnich, it then goes to the right over An Caisteal and the three peaks of Bidein Druim nan Ramh, to turn left again at Sgurr a'Mhadaidh. The distant serrated skyline sweeps over the southern section of the range and discloses the dominance of Sgurr Alasdair at its centre. Return to Sligachan the same way, but before dropping down into Fionn Choire, look at the Bhasteir Tooth, a weird overhanging obelisk of rock which soars skyward just below the *col.*

COIRE NA CREICHE. This corrie is a barren wilderness of rock and scree, but its architecture is on the grand scale and it is so near Sligachan as to be worthy of a visit. Follow the track by the Red Burn to the Bealach a 'Mhaim, then turn to the left and skirt the flank of the ridge running up to Bruach na Frithe. Descend the rough slopes and make for Sgurr an Fheadain, a small peak rising in the centre of the corrie and separating the two subsidiary corries of Mhadaidh and Tairneilear. Here you will find the famous Waterpipe Gully which splits Fheadain from top to bottom. This walk may be continued to Glen Brittle by picking up the track again below the Bealach a 'Mhaim and following it down to the rough mountain road which descends from Carbost.

COIRE LAGAN. This is the easiest walk from Glen Brittle, and most repaying to the novice, because it takes him right into the heart of the southern section of the Coolins. The track leading up to it is, perhaps, the most worn and the easiest to follow in the whole of the group. Leave the road at the bridge spanning the Allt Coire na Banachdich and follow the right bank of the burn, crossing it below the gorge. Here you take the path from Glen Brittle Lodge which meanders over the moor and bends back to the gorge opposite the Eas Mor Waterfall, one of the most lovely in the district. Thereafter, it rises gently round the long shoulder of Sgurr Dearg and passes Loch an 'Fhir-bhallaich on the right. Here it bifurcates, the right branch keeping more or less level and leading to the magnificent precipices of Sron na Ciche, and the left one following a mounting line of cairns skirting the slopes of Coire Lagan, whose steep glaciated façade of boulder plates is seen ahead. The scant vegetation gradually disappears as you climb, and after a steeper, twisting course you suddenly pass the last of the great boiler plates enclosing the lonely lochan in the bed of this wild corrie. Here you are surrounded by some of the grandest and most difficult peaks of the range: to the north is the shattered face of Sgurr Dearg, next to which leans the curious hump of An Stac, whose eastern face falls precipitously to the Bealach Coire Lagan. The skyline then rises to Sgurr Mhic Coinnich with its grim castellated summit, to fall again before the long sweep up to Sgurr Thearlaich, almost hidden by the pointed, dominating top of Sgurr Alasdair. A sharp drop carries the skyline down to the squarish bold summit of Sgurr Sgumain, which again merges with the gentler sloping flat top of Sron na Ciche.

Everywhere is desolation, with vast slopes of scree, caused by ages of rock disintegration, fanning out into the bottom of the corrie. In its basin rests the still, shallow waters of the lochan, where you may paddle or bathe to your heart's content. But if you walk over to the top of the gigantic, rounded boiler plate enclosing it, the seaward panorama stands out in stark contrast to this mountain wilderness. Below you lies the long arm of Loch Brittle with Rhum and Canna floating serenely on the surface of the rippling ocean, relieved here and there by the white sail of a ship, or the smoke trail of a steamer. The solitude and silence will profoundly impress you, the wisps of mist drifting in and out of the pinnacles and buttresses soaring into the sky in every direction, will fascinate you. And if you happen to be there in the stillness of a sunny evening, when the unflecked sky stretches from the sunrise to the sunset, you will want to linger by the smooth waters of this lochan. Whilst you watch and wait, the blue of the heavens will be slowly changed through every colour of the spectrum, and the setting sun will cast a soft shadow which mounts gradually over the glowing, pink crags, stretching upwards around you, until day passes into night. Then the jagged skyline will be silhouetted against the twinkling stars and you will stumble down the rough track back to Glen Brittle, perhaps in the ghostly light of the silvery moon, but with your being saturated with the magic and mystery of the incomparable Coolins.

AN CRUACHAN is the highest of the gently swelling hills which stand on the west of Glen Brittle. Covered with heather, bracken and bent, and rising above the long band of conifers planted by the Forestry Commission, they afford good views of the western corries of the Coolins and are comfortably crossed in a day.

SGURR NA BANACHDICH may be ascended by a variety of routes, but the easiest walk up to its summit is by skirting the base of Sgurr nan Gobhar which leads into Coir 'an Eich, and then following the burn to its source. An Diallaid rises on the left and a direct line is taken for its junction with Sgurr na Banachdich. A gentle scree walk follows until the cairn is attained. The precipices on the eastern side of its ridge are sensational, and the views of the northern section of the Main Ridge superb.

RUBH'AN DUNAIN is the south-westerly point of the peninsula, washed by the waters of Loch Brittle on the north, and by Soay

Sound on the south. The billowy moorland behind it stretches up to the flanks of the Coolins and is sprinkled with many a lochan from whose shores the corries are well seen in their proper perspective. The walk out to the Dun is the delight of a sunny afternoon. Its interest is increased by an inspection of the grand coast line whose promontories and caves, together with the hosts of sea birds which nest there, provide an excursion from Glen Brittle which should on no account be missed.

Easy routes for the scrambler

Readers of my numerous books devoted to the British Hills will know that I have had the unique experience of climbing most of them, traversing their airy ridges, studying their topography, and generally acquiring an intimate knowledge of their complex routes, dangers and difficulties. This aspect of mountaineering has convinced me that the experienced scrambler has far greater opportunities than the rock climber of appreciating the beauties of this type of country, because in taking the easier routes to the summits of the peaks he can visit a greater variety of viewpoints. The rock climber selects the more difficult ascents with the result that his time is often occupied by waiting on exposed, or deeply enclosed, belays, or by much of the other technique and routine of this admittedly thrilling sport. His movements are thus more strictly confined to viewpoints which are only slightly modified by altitude. I am, however, prepared to agree that a rope is necessary, and indeed essential if some of the sensational points on the Coolins are to be reached in safety. For instance I can scarcely imagine a solitary scrambler wandering up to the Cioch, although strangely enough one of them, who admitted his inexperience, related to me his risky climb to this amazing rock pinnacle!

When I speak of the experienced scrambler I mean anyone who has been roaming the mountains for years, who can roughly assess the feasibility of ascending or descending any obstacle that happens to be in his way, and who has learned to distinguish between the possible and the impossible according to his powers. Such a person, in fit condition, will discover a way to the summit

of most of the Coolins peaks without the aid of a rope, even if he
has to make a considerable detour to avoid an impasse. The
routes I shall describe in this monograph will help him in his
exploration but he should constantly bear in mind that route
finding in the Coolins is never easy in good weather, and under
bad conditions *needs the utmost concentration and a well
developed sense of direction.* As I have already said, the compass
is unreliable on many of these hills, and if the mist comes down
suddenly it is essential to remember which side of the ridge to
descend to safety. Many an experienced mountaineer has been
taught a lesson in Skye by finding himself at nightfall at the head
of Loch Coruisk, instead of near the comfortable hostels either at
Glen Brittle or Sligachan. Such a mistake involves miles of
walking over difficult ground round the coast or through Glen
Sligachan, and those who are wise beforehand will prepare for
the worst by carrying in their rucksacks not only a reserve of
food but a torch as well. Another useful instrument is a pocket
aneroid graduated in 100 feet (30·5 m) intervals up to 10,000 feet
(3048 m). When in difficulties this will indicate the height above or
below any known point, and in order to facilitate its application,
I give (p. 33) a classified list of the peaks in the order of their
altitude, as well as a similar list of the bealachs. In all cases I
have quoted the heights given to me by the Ordnance Survey
after they had fixed the correct altitudes by Stereo-comparator.

It will be seen from the list that there are 24 Munros in Skye.
Readers who are interested in this classification should refer to
my guidebook *The Scottish Peaks* or to the General Guide Book
of the Scottish Mountaineering Club.

The Coolins peaks in order of altitude

3,257 feet (993 m) Sgurr Alasdair
3,234 ,, (986 m) Inaccessible Pinnacle
3,209 ,, (978 m) Sgurr Dearg
3,208 ,, (977 m) Sgurr Thearlaich
3,192 ,, (973 m) Sgurr a' Greadaidh, North Top
3,181 ,, (970 m) Sgurr a' Greadiadh, South Top
3,167 ,, (965 m) Sgurr nan Gillean
3,166 ,, (965 m) Sgurr na Banachdich
3,143 ,, (958 m) Bruach na Frithe
3,125 ,, (952 m) An Stac
3,111 ,, (948 m) Sgurr Mhic Coinnich
3,108 ,, (947 m) Sgurr Sgumain
3,096 ,, (944 m) Sgurr Dubh Mor
3,089 ,, (942 m) Sgurr na Banachdich, Second Top
3,078 ,, (938 m) Sgurr Dubh na da Bheinn
3,069 ,, (935 m) Am Basteir
3,068 ,, (935 m) Sgurr a' Fionn Choire
3,044 ,, (928 m) Blaven, North Top
3,040 ,, (927 m) Sgurr Thormaid
3,032 ,, (924 m) Blaven, South Top
3,031 ,, (924 m) Sgurr nan Eag
3,023 ,, (922 m) Sgurr na Banachdich, Third Top
3,012 ,, (918 m) Sgurr a' Mhadaidh, south-west Peak
3,005 ,, (916 m) Bhasteir Tooth
2,951 ,, (899 m) Sgurr a' Bhasteir
2,950 ,, (899 m) Three Teeth
2,939 ,, (896 m) Sgurr a' Mhadaidh, Third Peak
2,935 ,, (895 m) Gars-bheinn
2,934 ,, (894 m) Sgurr a' Mhadaidh, north-west Peak
2,910 ,, (887 m) Sgurr a' Mhadaidh, Second Peak
2,885 ,, (879 m) Sgurr Thuilm
2,872 ,, (875 m) Sgurr a'Choire Bhig
2,850 ,, (869 m) Bidein Druim nan Ramh, Central Peak
2,826 ,, (861 m) Sgurr na Bhairnich
2,817 ,, (859 m) Sron na Ciche
2,794 ,, (852 m) Bidein Druim nan Ramh, North Peak
2,779 ,, (847 m) Bidein Druim nan Ramh, West Peak
2,730 ,, (832 m) An Caisteal
2,719 ,, (829 m) Caisteal a' Gharbh-Choire
2,644 ,, (806 m) Gharbh-bheinn
2,582 ,, (787 m) Clach Glas

2,525	,,	(770 m) Glamaig
2,511	,,	(765 m) Sgurr Beag
2,491	,,	(759 m) Sgurr Coire an Lochain
2,416	,,	(736 m) Sgurr nah 'Uamha
2,414	,,	(735 m) Marsco
2,403	,,	(732 m) Sgurr Dubh Beag
2,401	,,	(731 m) Beinn na Caillich
2,401	,,	(731 m) Beinne Dearg Mhor
2,350	,,	(716 m) Sgurr nan Each
2,325	,,	(709 m) Beinn Dearg Mhor, Broadford
2,300	,,	(701 m) An Diallaid
2,300	,,	(701 m) Belig
2,253	,,	(686 m) Sgurr an Fheadain
2,140	,,	(652 m) Beinn Dearg Mheadhonach
2,069	,,	(631 m) Sgurr nan Gobhar
2,012	,,	(613 m) Sron Dearg
1,916	,,	(584 m) Beinn Dearg Bheag, Broadford
1,871	,,	(570 m) Glas-Bheinn Mhor
1,670	,,	(509 m) Ciche na Beinn Deirge
1,631	,,	(497 m) Sgurr na Stri

The Coolins Bealachs in order of altitude

The Corries on the left of this table are all on the outside of the
Main Ridge whereas those on the right lead down to either Glen
Sligachan or Loch Coruisk. The Thearlaich-Dubh Gap is not a
Bealach although this break in the Main Ridge is at an altitude
of 2,950 feet (899 m) and thus higher than any of them.*

Coire Lagan	2,935 feet (895 m) Bealach Mhic Coinnich.	Coireachan Ruadha
Coire a'Ghreadaidh.	2,920 ,, (890 m) Bealach Thormaid.	Coireachan Ruadha
Fionn Choire	2,900 ,, (884 m) Bealach nan Lice	Lota Corrie
Coire na Dorus.	2,900 ,, (884 m) An Dorus	Coire an Uaigneis.
Coire na Dorus	2,890 ,, (881 m) Bealach Eag Dubh.	No exit.
Coir'a'Ghrunnda.	2,820 ,, (860 m) Bealach Coir'an Lochain.	Coir'an Lochain.
Coire na Banachdich.	2,791 ,, (851 m) Bealach Coire na Banachdich.	Coireachan Ruadha
Coire a'Bhasteir	2,733 ,, (834 m) Bealach Coir'a'Ghrunnda.	Lota Corrie.
Coire Lagan	2,735 ,, (833 m) Bealach a'Bhasteir.	Coir'a'Ghrunnda.*
Coire Lagan	2,655 ,, (809 m) Bealach Coire Lagan.	Coireachan Ruadha
Coir'a'Ghrunnda.	2,614 ,, (796 m) Bealach a'Gharbh-Choire.	An Garbh-Choire
Coire nan Laogh.	2,550 ,, (777 m) Bealach nan Eag	An Garbh-Choire.
Tairneilear.	2,492 ,, (760 m) Bealach na Glaic Moire.	Glac Mhor.

* This is the one exception since the Bealach Coir'a'Ghrunnda is on a lateral ridge.

In the preceding notes I have given prominence to Sligachan because I am convinced it is the best centre for walkers and for the initiation of newcomers to the geography of the Coolins. I am equally certain that Glen Brittle is the best centre for the scrambler and the rock climber because it lies in such close proximity to the scenes of their exploits. I shall, therefore, hereinafter describe the Main Ridge, its approaches and traverse, from south to north.

GARS-BHEINN TO SGURR NAN EAG. This part of the main Coolins ridge provides an entertaining scramble and may be traversed in either direction. In my opinion, it is better to climb the long scree slopes of Gars-bheinn and descend from Sgurr nan Eag to Coir'a'Ghrunnda, because the best views are ahead all the time. The former is a long, long way from Glen Brittle and is reached by following the track to Coire Lagan and leaving it as soon as the high moorland is reached. A direct line is taken for the shoulder of Sron na Ciche by passing Loch an'Fhir-bhallaich well on the left, then by skirting the flank of Sgurr nan Eag an oblique ascent is possible over the scree to the summit of Gars-bheinn, after crossing the Allt Coire nan Laogh fairly high up. The ridge undulates much more than it appears to do from a distance and, after passing the cairn of Sgurr nan Eag, a line is taken for the lochan in Coir'a'Ghrunnda. This is the most difficult part of the route because the face of the mountain is flecked by a number of glaciated slabs and there is no track, unless my own nail marks are still visible, in the disintegrated material lying between the boulders which are strewn almost everywhere!

COIR'A'GHRUNNDA. Follow the previous route but keep closer to the shoulder of Sron na Ciche and take a gradually rising diagonal course over it. You will then enter the corrie well above the stream issuing from it, and on bearing to the left will climb under the south-eastern face of the Sron, right into the left hand corner of the massive boiler plates. Here an easy scramble will bring you out on the edge of the lochan. Return to Coire Lagan by skirting the buttresses on the left and ascending the easy scree to the Bealach Coir'a'Ghrunnda. Here a cairn marks the top of the stone shoot, and when you get to the bottom of it, pick up the well-marked track below the Cioch which leads back to Glen Brittle.

SGURR SGUMAIN. It is not a long diversion to take in this summit on the previous scramble, but I do not recommend the descent of the vast scree slopes to the north of it. The easier course is to return to the Bealach. Sgumain is one of the most magnificent viewpoints in the south Coolins, so don't forget to take your camera.

SGURR ALASDAIR. Walk up to Coire Lagan and then ascend the Great Stone Shoot. Hug the rocks on the right until half way up where you pass a difficult bit, and then go over to the precipices on the left which make the ascent less arduous. An airy ridge rises to the right from the crest of the Shoot with sensational drops into its abysmal depths. The cairn stands on the smallest top in the Coolins and the views in all directions are superb. The descent is really trying and places a great strain on the knees and ankles, but do not endeavour to beat the alleged record of ten minutes. Run down the small scree in the centre of the Shoot and keep your body well back to avoid falling on your face.

SGURR DEARG. This is the nearest peak to Glen Brittle Lodge and the cairn on its summit ridge may be seen from the bedroom windows, just to the left of Sron Dearg. Follow the Coire Lagan track and on passing Eas Mor take a direct line for the great shoulder of the mountain. Make for a conspicuous dyke half way up and then keep to the ridge until you reach Sron Dearg. This is the castellated hill seen from afar and it is better to tackle it direct rather than go over to the right because this is no easier. On reaching the cairn the route follows the narrow ridge with sensational drops on the left, until it joins the broad summit ridge revealing commanding views, especially of the Alasdair group to the south. The Inaccessible Pinnacle is here disclosed in its true elevation, but do not try to scramble about on it alone, or you may become a casualty. Walk down the scree on the south side of it and scramble on to the summit of An Stac. This coign of vantage reveals its crest to advantage.

BEALACH COIRE NA BANACHDICH. This can be seen from Glen
Brittle as a narrow cleft in the ridge to the left below Sgurr Dearg
and affords the shortest approach to Loch Coruisk. Walk up to
the corrie by way of Eas Mor and on entering it note the
Window Buttress on the right. Pass round behind it and ascend
the loose scree gully in the flank of Sgurr Dearg. This gives access
to a series of broad ledges which are cairned but difficult to
follow in mist. The route rises to the left until the Bealach is
reached.

SGURR NA BANACHDICH. The most exhilarating ascent is by the
ridge of Sgurr nan Gobhar which leads straight up to the summit
of the mountain. Cross the moor from Glen Brittle, taking a
direct line for this shapely hill, and scramble up its shattered
slopes to the cairn which reveals its undulating ridge ahead with
Sgurr na Banachdich on the skyline. The crest of this lateral ridge
is a super Striding Edge with a few obstacles affording easy
scrambling. The final section is over boulders and scree, and the
summit cairn stands on the very edge of a sensational precipice
with terrific drops into the corrie far below. Those who do not
loiter too long by the way may traverse the Banachdich ridge to
Sgurr Dearg or vice versa.

SGURR A'GHREADAIDH occupies a superb position with an
unrivalled vista of Lock Coruisk backed by the sea, so its ascent
should be included in the programme of every scrambler. There
is only one easy way to its commanding summit and that is by
walking along the road to the Youth Hostel in Glen Brittle, and
then following the burn there to its source in Coire
a'Ghreadaidh. This stream comes down through a succession of
lovely ravines whose waterfalls make the route full of interest.
Once the vast wilderness of scree in the corrie has been reached,
it is best to take a line for the gap of Eag Dubh on the left of the
peak, and then to follow the rather indistinct track rising below
the crest of the ridge. A gigantic wart-like excrescence of rock will
be seen higher up, and on passing this, the north top of the
mountain appears ahead. Descend by the same route to Eag
Dubh and continue down the ridge to An Dorus, returning by
the ridge of Sgurr Thuilm.

SGURR THUILM AND SGURR A'MHADAIDH. As a high lateral ridge the former is conspicuous from all parts of Glen Brittle and is best approached by way of the burn mentioned in the last section. A tributary of this stream comes down on the left from the base of Sgurr Thuilm, and if this is followed to its source, an easy way will be found over the mountainous scree covering its slopes. Once the cairn is attained, the route is revealed along the crest of the ridge, the highest and most massive duplicate of the famous Striding Edge of Helvellyn in English Lakeland. The ridge is rough but easy and falls gently towards the gullied precipices of Sgurr a'Mhadaidh, disclosing wonderful views of the corries on either side as well as of the main ridge on the skyline. On reaching the *col* the cliffs ahead may be turned by taking to the scree on the right which leads to the narrow portals of An Dorus. A steep track on the left rises to the South West Peak of Sgurr a'Mhadaidh, whose summit affords a close view of the other three tops of this mountain. Experienced scramblers may conveniently combine the last two routes in either direction.

BEALACH NA GLAIC MOIRE is the last scramble that can be conveniently undertaken from Glen Brittle. It is also often accomplished from Sligachan. The pass lies between the North East Peak of Sgurr a'Mhadaidh and the West Peak of Bidein Druim nan Ramh. It gives access to Loch Coruisk for those making the round from the latter centre and returning to it by way of Glen Sligachan. Walkers from Glen Brittle skirt the slopes of Sgurr Thuilm to enter Coire na Creiche, and then scramble up the scree of Tairneiliar, hugging the flank of the lateral ridge of Sgurr an Fheadain which merges with the main ridge at Bidein. The Bealach is conspicuous on the skyline and reveals Loch Coruisk below. Walkers from Sligachan enter Coire na Creiche from the Bealach a'Mhaim and scramble up to the pass by way of Coir a'Mhadaidh, making first for the junction of the lateral ridge already referred to, and after crossing it, reaching the Bealach.

BRUACH NA FRITHE. As I have already stated this peak reveals the most comprehensive view of the bends in the main Coolins ridge, and whilst the scrambler may descend from its cairn by

way of Fionn Choire, he will surely climb it by the shattered
ridge of Tobar nan Uaislean running up to its summit from the
Bealach a'Mhaim. Cairns mark the commencement of this route,
the first part of which is at a gentle angle over scree-strewn
slopes, and the final section up steeper much broken rock. Those
who wish to take the easier course will keep to the sketchy track
on the Coire na Creiche side of the ridge, but the bold scrambler
will stick to its crest and enjoy the finer prospects on either side.

BEALACH NAN LICE. This is the high connecting link between
Fionn Choire and Lota Corrie and lies between the Bhasteir
Tooth and Sgurr a'Fionn Choire. It is used by those making the
circuit of the northern Coolins by way of Harta Corrie and Glen
Sligachan.

SGURR A'BHASTEIR is the shapely pyramid seen from Sligachan
on the right of Sgurr nan Gillean. Two shattered ridges support
its summit, that rising from the Am Basteir Gorge being longer
than the other falling to Meal Odhar on the west. Both of them
afford plenty of interesting scrambling and are approached by
the track which passes the Allt Dearg cottage. The cairn on the
summit reveals the finest spectacle of the Pinnacle Ridge of Sgurr
nan Gillean, away across the dark recesses of Coire a'Bhasteir,
with its tiny lochan far below. The traverse of this lateral ridge
may be combined with the ascent of Bruach na Frithe in either
direction.

BEALACH A'BHASTEIR is the easy pass lying between Am Basteir
and the Western Ridge of Sgurr nan Gillean. To reach it from
the Basteir Gorge involves a long toilsome ascent over some of
the roughest scree in the Coolins. Scramblers who wish to extend
their walk will enjoy the tricky traverse across the southern flank
of Sgurr nan Gillean which leads to the South-eastern ridge of
this mountain. By descending the Tourist Route they will
accomplish the circuit of this peak.

SGURR NAN GILLEAN is a favourite climb with all scramblers
because the thrill of height is so easily experienced during the
ascent of the South-eastern ridge of this mountain. The well
known Tourist Route leaves the Sligachan Hotel at its power-
house, and after crossing the bridge nearby, gradually rises

across the moor until it reaches the Allt Dearg Beag. This is crossed at any convenient spot and a way made over the trackless bog to a gap in the low ridge of Nead na h'Iolaire. Here a cairn marks the commencement of the path through Coire Riabhach where its lochan is passed on the left. Thereafter the track steepens and is well cairned right up to the South-eastern ridge. The real scramble now begins and the easier ascent is on the Lota Corrie side of the ridge but the last hundred feet cannot be avoided and is the most sensational part of the climb. The summit cairn is built upon a small platform which is perhaps the most isolated in all the Coolins. Unless the scrambler has had considerable climbing experience it is safest to descend by the same route when he may walk down the ridge to Sgurr Beag and Sgurr na h'Uamha before returning to his hotel.

The main Coolins Ridge

The traverse of this ridge is famous throughout the mountaineering world and calls for greater experience, concentration and strength, coupled with a sureness of foot and eye, than any other of the well known ridges in the country. The map distance from Glen Brittle to Sligachan by way of Gars-bheinn and Sgurr nan Gillean is about fifteen miles (25 km) and involves some 10,000 feet (3048 m) of ascent and descent. Quite a number of climbers have made the traverse in sections in the course of a holiday, but those who have accomplished it completely in one day are a select few. The pioneers of this expedition were Messrs. M'Laren and Shadbolt who left Glen Brittle at 3.35 a.m. on 10 June 1911. They reached Gars-bheinn in two and a half hours, and after spending twelve and one-third hours traversing the ridge, descended from Sgurr nan Gillean in two hours to arrive at Sligachan at 8.20 p.m. In 1914, Mr. T. Howard Somervell completed a solitary traverse in much faster time by arriving at Sgurr na h'Uamha at the end of the ridge in ten and a half hours. Since then it has been accomplished by a number of women as well as men, but the record is held by Mr. P. Bicknell, whose time from Glen Brittle to Sligachan was just under twelve hours. He made the traverse in August 1932, spent

eight hours on the ridge ending at Sgurr nan Gillean, and halted
to rest for one hour only—a marvellous performance.

This record remains to be broken, and it will require some
doing, but in June 1939 the Main Ridge *and* Blaven were
traversed for the first time in one day by I. G. Charleson and
W. E. Forde.

The first winter traverse of the Main Ridge in heavy snow was
made in February 1965 by Patey, Robertson, Crabb and
MacInnes. They took two days to complete it, going south from
Gillean, and made a bivouac on Banachdich where food had
previously been deposited, brought up from Glen Brittle.

The Magic of Skye is not intended as a guide to this traverse
although many climbers will doubtless find it helpful. Such a
book was first published by the Scottish Mountaineering Club as
long ago as 1923 and has since run into three editions. It not only
covers this ground admirably but also includes full details of all
the other well known courses in the Coolins. Moreover, it has a
small format and is thus easily carried in the climber's rucksack
for ready reference.

There are a few points in this volume, however, which call for
comment because they are the subject of much disagreement
among those who know these hills intimately. For instance, the
times allowed for a climber to get home from several of the
frequented places are open to considerable doubt, unless, of
course, they are based upon the performance of a well-trained
athlete in first class condition. During my present sojourn at
Glen Brittle Lodge I had the privilege of climbing with a number
of tough and experienced young men, and while we were never
out to break any records, we found it impossible to make some
of the times given without *running* down the hills. There are very
few people who are sure-footed enough to do this sort of thing
without breaking an ankle, especially since the average person
takes only one or two short holidays a year and is thus not in
perfect training. To make a modest estimate, I would say that
these times need to be increased by about fifty per cent to give
most people sufficient margin to get home safely in clear weather.

The 1,300 feet (396 m) of scree which constitutes the Great

Stone Shoot of Sgurr Alasdair is well known to most of those who visit the Coolins. It consists mainly of large stones, although in the centre near the bottom they are smaller and thus run more easily. The average person takes at least half-an-hour to descend it, whereas the S.M.C. Guide says it is *possible* to come down in 15 minutes. The fittest of the Good Companions was timed over this course, and by *running down at full tilt* he made the bottom in 14 minutes, much to our surprise.

Elsewhere in this volume there are statements about the times taken to ascend and descend Glamaig from the Sligachan Inn. Most of us have heard of the record set up by an Indian who was taken to Skye by the late General Bruce of Everest fame. He is reputed to have climbed this great cone of granite in 37 minutes and to have come back again to the hotel in 18 minutes. This feat, however, is not likely to be repeated; but in another place in this guide the time for the ascent is given as 80 minutes and the descent as 40 minutes. While staying at Sligachan on the present occasion, several of the hardier walkers climbed Glamaig, and as there was such a wide difference in their performances, I timed myself one afternoon on the same course. Starting from the road beside Loch Sligachan I ascended the north-west face of the mountain to avoid as much scree as possible and reached the summit in one and a quarter hours without stopping for a rest. Had I taken a direct line from the hotel over the moor it would have taken at least another half hour to attain the cairn.

The classification of the climbs is another moot point and has already occupied the attention of the editors of this excellent volume. After consulting a number of experts they admit there is a tendency to over-rate the difficulties of the courses in the light of modern rock-climbing technique. It would, of course, require the criticism of an acknowledged expert who knows them all to provide a really reliable reclassification, and as I personally know so few of them, my opinion cannot be taken too seriously. There are, however, some of the classifications I found misleading and I give my comments here for what they are worth.

Sgurr Alasdair by the South-west ridge from Sgumain. If this is taken direct there is only one difficult bit which is known as the *mauvais pas*. It is classified as 2, Moderate, which means that a rope is advisable except in the case of experienced climbers. Those who are familiar with it will remember that the corner overhangs and has only a few sloping holds. All the Good Companions looked at it, some attempted it, but only one succeeded in climbing this tricky obstruction. One of us had seen a leader come to grief on a previous occasion and I understand he was not the first to break an ankle here.

Sron na Ciche by the Eastern Gully. The Second Pitch is the crux of this course and consists of a jammed boulder and cave which has never been climbed direct. It is usually turned on the left wall of the gully by ascending a crack, crossing a ledge, and finishing by a short hand traverse which leads to the top of the pitch. This is classified as 3, Difficult, and suitable for experienced climbers using a rope. Two of us scaled this on our way to the Cioch and we came to the conclusion that it was easier than the *mauvais pas* on Alasdair.

Sgurr nan Gillean, Nicolson's Chimney. This is usually taken in the descent and is stated to be a 'rake' which provides an easy route off the Western Ridge. It is classified as 1, Easy, where a rope is unnecessary under ordinary conditions. The last part of this sentence is the saving feature of this classification because as every mountaineer knows, courses which are easy in good weather may be impracticable at other times, or at least in another category. On the present occasion I descended the Western Ridge alone and with a rucksack: it was raining which made the rocks wet and slippery, so that when I came down to the vertical section of this chimney it called upon all my powers to descend it in safety. Basing my opinion upon the Rakes of English Lakeland which I know well, I consider the above description of it to be at least misleading; it is just a short chimney and an awkward one too. I discussed the point with a Portree resident who has climbed regularly in the Coolins for some years. He has opportunities of going there in all weathers and is very familiar with this terrain. He agrees with me that of the two routes off the Western Ridge of Sgurr nan Gillean, Nicolson's is more difficult than the usual one over the

'Policeman', and yet the former is graded as 1, and the latter as 2.

Returning now to the more detailed topography of the Main Ridge, I have tabulated its principal features on p. 46 for easy reference. Those who do not wish to make the traverse by adhering strictly to its crest may save much time by turning some of the difficult bits on one side or the other. For instance, the Inaccessible Pinnacle on Sgurr Dearg can be easily turned on the south side, whereas the Thearlaich-Dubh Gap cannot be avoided unless the Main Ridge is deserted and the scree crossed to the Alasdair-Sgumain col. Sgurr Thearlaich may, however, be regained, but only by traversing Alasdair and the crest of the Great Stone Shoot.

Topography of the main ridge

Height in feet	Feature	Remarks	Lateral ridges
2,935 (895 m)	Gars-bheinn	Rough crest	
2,760 (841 m)	Dip		
2,872 (875 m)	Sgurr a'Choire Bhig	No difficulties	N.E. Branch
2,550 (857 m)	Bealach		
3,031 (924 m)	Sgurr nan Eag	Scrambling at the north end where ridge falls to bealach	
2,620 (912 m)	Bealach a'Gharbh-choire		
2,740 (835 m)	Caisteal a'Gharbh-choire	Rock-climbing but may be turned on either side	
2,620 (912 m)	Dip		
3,078 (938 m)	Sgurr Dubh an Da Bheinn	Scrambling to summit, but may be traversed on west	East branch over Sgurr Dubh Mor, 3,096 feet (944 m); and Sgurr Dubh Beag, 2,403 feet (732 m); descent to Loch Coruisk
2,820 (860 m)	Bealach Coir'an Lochain		
2,980 (908 m)	Pinnacle	Steep scramble	
2,806 (855 m)	Thearlaich-Dubh Gap	Rock climb; cannot be turned without	

Height in feet	Feature	Remarks	Lateral Ridges
3,208 (977 m)	Sgurr Thearlaich	Good scramble to summit; ridge to bealach narrow and sensational	N.E. Branch to Sgurr Coire an Lochain, 2,480 feet (734 m); S.W. Branch over Stone shoot, 1,300 feet (396 m); Alasdair, 3,257 feet (993 m); Sgumain, 3,108 feet (947 m); Sron na Ciche, 2,817 feet (859 m)
2,935 (895 m)	Bealach Mhic Coinnich		
3,111 (948 m)	Sgurr Mhic Coinnich	Rock climbing; narrow ridge	
2,655 (809 m)	Bealach Coire Lagan		
3,125 (952 m)	An Stac	Rock climb, steep face; can be turned on S.W. side	
3,234 (986 m)	Inaccessible Pinnacle	Rock climb, exposed; may be turned on south side	
3,209 (978 m)	Sgurr Dearg	Easy walk down to bealach	West branch narrow to Sron Dearg 2,012 feet (613 m)

Height in feet	Feature	Remarks	Lateral ridges
2,791 (851 m)	Bealach Coire na Banachdich		
3,166 (965 m)	Sgurr na Banachdich	Good scramble, easier on west side of crest. Sharp drop to bealach	
2,920 (890 m)	Bealach Thormaid		
3,040 (927 m)	Sgurr Thormaid	Good scramble	
2,925 (892 m)	Dip		
2,950 (899·9 m)	Three Teeth	Scramble, may be turned on west	
2,780 (847 m)	Dip		
3,181 (970 m)	Sgurr A'Ghreadaidh, south top	Good scramble, narrow ridge to north top	
3,192 (973 m)	Sgurr a'Ghreadiadh, north top	Easy descent	S.W. spur
2,890 (881 m)	Eag Dubh	Narrow gap in ridge, easily passed	
2,900 (884 m)	An Dorus	Vertical descent of 20 feet (6·06 m)	

Height	Peak	Description	Ridge/Branch
3,012 (918 m)	Sgurr a'Mhadaidh, S.W. peak	Good scramble, also to next top, 2,925 feet (892 m); thereafter rock climbing over two more tops, 2,907 feet (886 m); 2,935 feet (895 m)	N.W. branch to Sgurr Thuilm, 2,885 feet (879 m)
2,510 (765 m)	Bealach na Glaic Moire		
2,850 (869 m)	Bidein Druim nan Ramh, Central Peak	Highest of three tops, north 2,790 feet (850.3 m); west 2,780 feet (847 m); rock-climbing over them all	S.E branch, Druim nan Ramh terminating with Sgurr na Stri, 1,631 feet (497 m)
2,510 (765 m)	Bealach		
2,730 (832 m)	An Caisteal		
2,520 (768 m)	Gash	Scrambling	
2,826 (867 m)	Sgurr na Bhairnich	Scrambling, may be turned by ledge on west side	
3,143 (952 m)	Bruach na Frithe	Easy scrambling	N.W. branch to Sron an Tobar nan Uaislean, 1,682 feet (513 m)
3,068 (935 m)	Sgurr a'Fionn Choire	Good scramble, may be turned on N.W. side	

Height in feet	Feature	Remarks	Lateral ridges
2,900 (884 m)	Bealach nan Lice		
3,005 (916 m)	Bhasteir Tooth	Rock climb, turned on north side	North branch to Sgurr a'Bhasteir, 2,950 feet (899 m)
3,069 (935 m)	Am Basteir	Rock climb, turned on north side by steep scree	
2,733 (833 m)	Bealach a'Bhasteir		
3,167 (965 m)	Sgurr nan Gillean	Rock climb up Western Ridge, good scramble down S.E. Ridge	Pinnacle Ridge branches N.N.E. lowest top, 2,500 feet (762 m)
2,511 (765 m)	Sgurr Beag	Easy scramble	
2,416 736 m)	Sgurr na h'Uamha	Sensational scramble with two pitches	

The phantasmagoria of the past, which lends romance to the Misty Isle, is merged in the general history of the Highlands, and the numerous writers who have given accounts of its racial wars and clan battles fought here and there on its windy moors, together with its opposition to the Scottish Kings, make up a tale which has fascinated readers for decades.

Certain phases of this long story emerge more clearly from the dim halo which surrounds the island, and whilst it is not the purpose of this book to recount in detail the facts and fancies that have provided the theme of many a distinguished author, a few of the more important epochs which mark its history are cited here. Readers who wish to delve into this glamorous past can consult the vast literature already devoted to it.

1. *The Celts.* Many of the mythical heroes of this era are supposed to have played their part in shaping the destinies of Skye and their names are yet remembered. Cuchullainn of the Ossianic Poems was the island chief, with his seat at Dunskaith near Ord in Sleat. He went to the Irish Wars, leaving behind his fair wife Bragela, but he never returned. Fingal visited the island and organised a great deer drive in Strath when six thousand deer were slain. According to tradition this hero used to sit on Fingal's Seat above Portree where he often directed the chase in the valley below.

2. *St. Columba.* The coming of this Saint doomed the paganism of the Celts whose custom it had been, under the priesthood of the Druids, to mingle magic with religious rites and often with the sacrifice of human victims. St. Columba arrived from Iona in 565 AD and with his monks set out to Christianise this heathendom. He was wonderfully successful.

3. *The Scandinavian Conquest.* The complete domination of the Isles by the Norsemen took place by the end of the ninth century, but in the preceding years these born adventurers had fought, ravaged, plundered and killed the natives in their frequent raids. Their occupation of the Hebrides was almost continuous throughout the tenth, eleventh and twelfth centuries, but they

were defeated by Somerled, first in 1156 off Isla, and again in 1158 when he became the first Lord of the Isles, a title which his descendants still hold. Somerled was a strong and ruthless ruler but after his death in 1164, his sons could not hold their own against the Scandinavians whose dominion continued to run its course.

The Scottish Kings now began to take more interest in these rivals who disputed their overlordship of the Western Isles, and after several encounters with them, Alexander III attempted to negotiate the purchase of the Isles from Haco. This Norseman, however, declined the invitation, and instead, mustered a fleet in July, 1263, and sailed first to Lewis and then to Kyleakin where he picked up reinforcements. In the meantime, Alexander III had also been mustering his forces and the opposing sides met at Largs where a great battle was fought. This was the beginning of Haco's end, for in escaping with his galleys, he was overwhelmed by a hurricane which wrecked much of his fleet on the coast of Lorne, Mull and Skye. He took refuge in Loch Bracadale and afterwards set sail for home, but landed at Kirkwall where he died, thus ending the days of Norse domination of the Isles of the West.

Strangely enough the Celtic tongue was not affected by the Scandinavian occupation although in the Misty Isle there are many Norse place names, such as the -bosts and the -vaigs, but these may be the mere equivalents of the earlier Celtic nomenclature.

4. *Submission to the Scottish Kings*. With the defeat of the Norsemen, the Lords of the Isles and their Chieftains held their lands from the Scottish Kings as feudal superiors, but during the next two centuries they disputed this vassalage by rebellion against the throne and by bloody feuds among themselves. They were, however, finally defeated and reduced to submission to the Scottish Crown by James IV and James V and it was the latter's visit to Skye that again brought this island into prominence. He mustered a great fleet which sailed from the Firth of Forth and finally reached Loch Dunvegan by way of the Orkneys and the Outer Isles. Here Alexander, the chief of the clan, was made

prisoner, and the ships then sailed round to Score Bay where the King visited Duntulm Castle, at that time occupied by the son of Donald Gorme who had previously ejected the Macleods. The fleet then sailed down Raasay Sound and entered Portree Bay where they dropped anchor. The King, his retinue, and his army landed on the rocky shore and there, with much pomp and pageantry, received the island chiefs and their followers as proof of their submission to the crown and its superior forces. James V, like most of the Stuarts, was a student of human nature and there seems little doubt his great expedition effected what centuries of fighting had failed to do. He returned homewards by Kylerhea and the Firth of Clyde and died in 1542.

5. *The Wanderings of Prince Charlie* provide one of the most romantic episodes of the Misty Isle, and coupled with the devotion of Flora Macdonald, make up a story that will live through the ages. This glamorous young man raised his standard at Glenshiel, and in anticipation of aid from the chieftains of Skye, sent Clanranald there to plead his cause, only to find after meeting Macdonald and MacLeod at Sconser, that they were unwilling to help him. The clansmen of Skye were mustered by their chiefs but on discovering that they were to fight against the Prince, most of them deserted and went off to join him.

After Culloden, Prince Charlie wandered, hunted and homeless, eventually to arrive at Glenboisdale whence he was taken by boat to Benbecula, and afterwards to Lewis and South Uist. Months of wandering followed until he and his followers found themselves gradually surrounded by their opponents both on land and sea. It was in this grave hour of need that Flora Macdonald came to his rescue. She was staying at the time with her brother in South Uist and it was suggested she should escort the Prince to her home at Armadale in Skye. She met him on the night of 21st June, 1746, and after making the necessary arrangements for his disguise as Betty Burke, her Irish servant, they left Rossinish together by boat. An unsuccessful attempt was made to land at Vaternish Point so they crossed the mouth of Loch Snizort and disembarked near Monkstadt, a seat of the Macdonalds. Kingsburgh was staying there at the time, and while Flora dined with Lady Margaret, he took provisions to the Prince who was waiting on the hillside nearby. Later the party left for Kingsburgh House, and after arriving there safely, the Prince retired to enjoy the luxury of a bed. It was during his sojourn here that he allowed Flora to 'cut a lock frae his long yellow hair,' a trifling incident perhaps, but one of such romantic devotion as will live through the pages of history. The party ultimately left this refuge in drenching rain, and after discarding his disguise in a wood some distance from the house, the Prince proceeded towards Portree en route for Raasay with a boy as guide. In due course he reached the inn, now known as the Royal Hotel, and after obtaining refreshment but no silver change for his guinea, he took leave of Flora Macdonald and slipped away to meet his Raasay supporters. They all embarked in a boat which had been laboriously secured from Loch Fada below the Storr, and set sail for Raasay where the Prince lay in hiding for two days. He then returned to Skye, and after all his followers had left him, save the faithful Malcolm MacLeod, set out for Strath as the latter's servant, with a bottle of brandy to sustain them on the long trudge over the most difficult ground on the island. They made a roundabout journey over the hills by way of Loch Ainort ultimately to arrive at the house of the Mackinnons in Elgol, where the aged chief was fetched to meet the Prince. He was led to a cave near the south-east end of Loch Scavaig which still bears the Royal name, and after taking refuge there for some days, left it by boat for the mainland at 8 p.m. on Friday, July 4th in the company of two Mackinnons. The party reached Mallaig after a rough crossing and Prince Charlie then continued his wanderings until September 20th, when he was able to embark for France. Thus ended the Highland journey of one who fought and failed with such good grace that his memory is cherished throughout the Magic Isle.

6. *The discovery of Skye*. With the passing of Culloden and the cessation of strife between the clans, life in Skye became more peaceful, and travellers from the south were induced to visit this wild region of the north-west. The arrival of Pennant in 1772 and of Dr. Johnson and his faithful Boswell in 1773 marks the

beginning of this new era; before this southerners regarded the Highlanders as a barbarous race and had thus little inclination to make a long and trying journey to explore their country. The publication of Johnson's *Journey* and Boswell's *Tour* exploded these erroneous ideas and thereafter a gradually increasing stream of wayfarers penetrated the fastnesses of the Western Highlands and of Skye. Forty years later Sir Walter Scott sailed round the north of Scotland in the Light-house yacht, and after visiting Harris, dropped anchor in Loch Dunvegan on the 23rd August, 1814. Two days later he left for Loch Scavaig and paid his famous visit to Loch Coruisk to which he did due justice in his subsequent diary and poem.

Since then the popularity of Skye has increased by leaps and bounds, and among those who have contributed to it are such distinguished writers as Alexander Smith whose *Summer in Skye* appeared in 1865, and later Canon J. A. MacCulloch who in 1905 published his *Misty Isle of Skye*, a work which for sheer beauty of descriptive prose is unrivalled. Seton Gordon, the eminent naturalist, wrote widely in praise of the island and loved it so much that he went to live there.

Some years earlier than this, the Coolins attracted the attention of the mountaineer who soon realized the remarkable possibilities of this spectacular terrain as a field for every type of rock gymnastics: it is marked by the classic work of Ashley P. Abraham whose *Rock Climbing in Skye* appeared in 1908.

The painter has also found this island rich in subjects for his brush and canvas, and Ruskin and Turner were the forerunners of a long line of artists whose pictures have charmed the eye of thousands. In this direction the Coolins have not been neglected and the paintings of Eyre Walker and Cecil A. Hunt in particular are constantly admired by climbers.

After these glowing tributes to almost every beautiful aspect of Skye, this volume may seem superfluous, but strangely enough with perhaps the one exception of Canon MacCulloch's book, the rest of the literature touches upon individual facets only of its wonderful beauty in which both the Storr and Quiraing seem to have been sadly overlooked. There are some who will say that the unerring eye of the modern camera still fails to capture the moods and subtleness of this strange Hebridean loveliness, but if these studies together with the descriptive text reveal a small part of its charm, then others may be persuaded to go there and steep themselves in magic.

Place-names of Skye have always been an enigma to the Sassenach because their spelling is frequently obscure and their correct pronunciation most perplexing. When it is realised for instance that Mhadaidh is pronounced *Vatee*, or Thuilm *Hulim*, it will be obvious that unless the speaker is familiar with the Gaelic tongue he is scarcely ever understood by the native. The position, however, is further complicated by the number of apparently correct spellings for one and the same place. The Coolins, for example, may be spelt Cuillin, Culinn, Cuillfhionn, Cuildhean, Cuilionn, Culluchin, Gulluin, Quillin, Cullin and Cuchullin. I have adopted the first one throughout this work and I have no doubt Gaelic scholars, and especially Scots living south of the Border, who often presume to know much about the subject, will say I should have selected one of the others. I take no responsibility for this choice, however, because I see that noted Scottish writers have done the same thing and I am therefore in good company!

It is probable that tens of thousands of English and Welsh people will read this book in addition to the thousands of Scots who should glow with pride at the publicity I am giving their finest piece of scenery. Whilst they may be familiar with all the intricacies of the Skye Place-Names I think it will be helpful to others, and at least clarify the position so far as this volume is concerned, if I give some authentic information about them. I have therefore taken as my authority the work of Alexander Robert Forbes whose *Place-Names of Skye* is the most lucid and detailed exposition on the whole problem. I have adopted the more usually accepted spellings throughout the text where I have given neither the English nor Welsh meaning nor the pronunciations. The following list should in consequence provide such information as is usually sought on these matters.

ABHAINN, ABHUINN, AMHAINN, AMHUINN. A river.

AIRD, AIRDE, AN AIRDE, NA H'AIRDE. The height or heights, points or promontories.

ALLT. A river or burn, with high or precipitous banks.

AMAR (river). The trough or river of the rocky channel. Old Highlanders used this word for a pot.

ASHIG, AISEAG, AISHIG, ASHAIG. The crossing, the ferry.

ATH NA GLAISSICH, GLAISEACH. Ford of the foam.

BAC-NA-H'UAMHA. Cave ridge. At back of Garbh-Bheinn.

BAGHAN. A little bay, a local harbour.

BARPA. A barrow, a cairn.

BASADAIR, AM BASTEIR. The Executioner, probably in reference to the outline of the Bhasteir Tooth, which some consider resembles a headsman's axe.

BEAL, BEUL, BIAL, BIEL. Mouth. This is a common pasturage and lair or lying place for cattle.

BEALACH, BELLACH, BALLACH, BALLOCH. A pass.

BEALACH A'BHAISTEIR (BHASTEIR). Pass of the Executioner.

BEALACH A BHORBHAIN, BHORBHEIN, MHORMHAIN, MHORBHEINN. A pass between Storr and Quiraing.

BEALACH A BHUIRIDH. Belig. Pass of the bellowing stags.

BEALACH ACHADH NAN GOBHAR. Torrin. Pass of the goats' field.

BEALACH A CHLAIB. The wide-mouth pass. Also a battlefield.

BEALACH A CHOISICHE. The traveller or pedestrian's pass, a footpath.

BEALACH A CHUIRN. Cairns' pass.

BEALACH A GHLAS-CHOIRE. Green corrie pass. Between Sgurr Beag and Sgurr na h'Uamha.

BEALACH A LEITIR (NAN LICE), pron. *Leeka*, the hill-side pass. Pass of the Flat Stones. Between Fionn Choire and Lota Corrie.

BEALACH A MHAIM (*màm*, a rounded hill). Pass of the round hill, between Sligachan and Glen Brittle.

BEALACH A MHOR-AMHAIN, -ABHAINN. Pass of the great river, near Beinn Mheadhonach, Trotternish.

BEALACH AN LEACAICH. Flat stones' pass. *Leacach* means the bare summit of a hill.

BEALACH AN SCARD. Scree pass. There are so many of them in the Coolins that the term *Bealachan, or Bealaichean* rather, has been given to all.

BEALACH 'CHARRA or A CHARRA. Pass of the rock, or rocky ledge.

BEALACH COIRE NAN ALLT GEALA. Pass of the corrie of the white burns (clear). Between Sgurr nan Gillean and Sgurr Beag.

BEALACH COIRE-SIONNAICH. Fox-corrie pass.

BEALACH GARBH. Rough Pass.

BEALACH HARTAVAL. Harta-fell pass, in or among the Coolins.

BEALACH MHARSCO. Marsco pass.

BEALACH MHIC-COINNICH. Mackenzie's pass—a famous guide to the Coolins.

BEALACH NA COISE. The footpath;

also *Bealach a Choisiche*.
Between Coruisk and Coire na
Creiche.

BEALACH NA GLAICE-MOIRE. Pass of
the great defile or hollow.
Between Bidein Druim nan
Ramh and Sgurr a'Mhadiadh.

BEALACH NAN LICE. See Bealach a
Leitir.

BEALACH-NA-SGAIRDE. The pass of
the scree.

BEALACH UIG. Uig pass, just south
of Quiraing.

BEANN, BEINN, BEN. The primary
meaning of *ben* is horn, hence
peak. In Scotland the term in
the oblique form, *beinn*, is
extended to apply to any hill,
without regard to shape,
though traces of the old usage
are common. The diminutive
binnean always denotes a peaked
hill, sometimes by no means
diminutive in size. A mountain
is a mountain in England, but
when the climber is in Scotland
it may be a *beinn*, a *creag*, or a
meall, a *spidean* or *sgor*, a *carn*
or *monadh*, a *stùc* or a *torr*.
According to the late Professor
J. Geikie, 'It is impossible to
distinguish clearly between hills
and mountains; in general, a hill
is properly restricted to more or
less abrupt elevations of less
than 1,000 feet—*monadh*,
monaidhean—all the altitudes
exceeding this being
mountains—*beanntan* or
beannta—though eminences
considerably above 1,000 feet
are often spoken of as hills, as
the Coolins are in English.'

BEINN BELIG, BEILIG, BEILEAG,
BHELIG. *Beileach* means birch-
tree bark. This mountain, like
several others, does not have
'Beinn' prefixed. Strath.

BEINN DEANAVAIG, DIANAVAIG,
TIANAVAIG, TIANABHAIG. The hill
or mountain of the stormy bay.
Also 'Inivaig,' hill or mountain
of protection or defiance (of the
elements). Also 'the hill of his
defence.' Opposite Portree.

BEINN EDRA, EADARA, ETHRA,
EADARAINN. The hill between
others—Storr and Quiraing.

BEINN MHEADHONACH. Mid or
middle mount.

BEINN NA CAILLICH. Literally, the
old woman's mountain. It is
near Broadford and said to be
named after a Norwegian or
Danish Princess (or her nurse),
whose remains are interred on
the summit.

BELIG, BEILIG. A mountain in
Strath. See 'Beinn Belig.'

BEUL, BEAL, BIAL A CHREAG MHOR.
Mouth or opening of the great
rock. North Harbour, Portree.

BIDEAN, or AM BIODAN, which
signifies a hedge or fence, but
thought meant for *bidein*, a
sharp point, a summit, a
pinnacle.

BIDEIN DRUIM NAN RAMH. The
summit of the ridge of the roots,
whence the Coolins radiate. The
'hub' of the range.

BIDEIN NA H-IOLAIRE. The eagle's
pinnacle or perching place.

BIL, BILE, AM. The verge or edge of
a precipice.

BLAVEN, BLABHEINN, BLATH-

BHEINN. The hill of bloom, the warm or sunny mount, from red appearance, the blue wild mountain. *Flath-bheinn*, the Heroes Mount.

BODHA, AM. The sunk rock, or submerged rock or reef.

BRACADALE, BRACADOLL. The spotted dale. May be brakendale or ferndale. Said to mean also open place for meeting of township.

BRUACH NA FRITHE, BRUTHACH NA FREE. Pron. *Bruach na Free*. The brae of the forest, heath, moor or slope.

BUAILE. Cattle fold.

BUGH or BUGHA. A green spot or peninsula formed by the winding of a river.

CACHLAIDH RUADH. Red or russet pass.

CADHA NAN EACH. Pass of the horses.

CADHA NAN INGREAN, INGHINN, NIGHINN. Pass of the young girl. On shore of Loch Slapin.

CAILLEACH, A CHAILLEACH, or CLACH-A-CHAILLICH. The Old Wife; sometimes spelt *kailleach*, the hill of the roaring blast.

CAISTEAL MAOL, MAOIL, CAISTEAL A MHAOIL. Castle Moil, on a bare promontory at Kyleakin, also named Dunakyne.

CAMUS A MHOR BHEOIL. The bay of the great mouth, opposite the narrows of Portree.

CAMUS A MHURAN, A MHURAIN. Bay of the sea-bent. At Rudh'an Dunain.

CAMUSUNARY, CAMUSIUNARIE, CAMUSMARY, CAMASUNARY. Bay of the white or fair or beautiful

sheiling. Locally, the late or dark bay. Possibly the Bay of Watching.

CANNA, CANA. The little whale or porpoise from the shape of the island.

CARBOST, CARABOST. A mossy place.

CEALLAICHEAN, NA. Rocks, or ravines in inland rocks which can be climbed.

CEANN NA BEINNE. Head of the mountain. East of Loch Brittle.

CEUM CARACH, CORRACH, or AN CEUM SLEAMHUINN. The risky bad, or slippery step; also the Ladies Step on the shore track round Loch Scavaig, from Camasunary.

'CHUILIONN. The Hollies. The Coolins.

CICHE NA BEINNE DEIRGE. The pinnacle or breast of the red mountain.

CIOCH A SGUMAIN. The pap or breast of the Sguman. The Cioch is now known universally as the conspicuous boss of rock projecting from the face of Sron na Ciche.

CIREAN THORMAID. Norman's ridge or crest, after the late Norman Collie who explored much of the Coolins.

CLACHAN. A hamlet or village with church and burying ground.

CLACH AN FHUARAIN. The well or fountain stone; said to have been thrown hither from the island of Soay, four and a half miles distant, by one of the 'Cuchullin' giants when indulging in the pastime of 'putting' the stone! It is estimated to weigh two tons and is doubtless one of the many 'travelled' relics of the Ice Age. It lies near Elgol.

CLACH CHROTACH. The crooked or bent stone in Staffin.

CLACH FUILEACH or FUILTEACH. The bloody stone in Harta Corrie. Colour probably due to the presence of pyrites.

CLACH GLAS, GHLAS. The grey stone. The prominent massive tower to the north of Blaven. Sometimes known as the 'Matterhorn of Skye.'

CLEAT, CLEIT, CLEITE, CLEITEADH, CLETT, CLAIT. An isolated rock, a cliff, a ridge of rocks in the sea.

CNAP, AN. The lump. A hill above Portree harbour.

CNAP AN ROIN. The seal's lump or hillock. In Portree Loch.

CNOC. A knoll.

COILEACH GLAMAIG. The cock, peak, crest, or summit of Glamaig. An Coileach is in fact the eastern summit of the mountain, the highest top being named Sgurr Mhairi—Mary's Peak.

COIRE. A corrie or coomb, combe or cwm. A more or less circular hollow in the side of a hill.

COIR' A CHROIN. Rutting corry.

COIR' A CHRUIDH. Corry of the cows. East of Garsbheinn.

COIR' A GHRUNNDA. Corry of the ground. This corry has been found given as 'Coire Ghrannda,' the nasty, ugly, awesome corry, but *granda* is the correct spelling; the latter meaning 'the wildest and most savage of all.'

COIREACHAN RUADHA. The red corries beneath Sgurr a' Ghreadaidh.

COIR' AM FRAOCH or FROACH CHOIRE. The heather or heathery corry. Locally said to be the 'Corry of the shields.' It lies between Marsco and Ruadh Stac.

COIR'A MHADAIDH. The dog or wolf's corry. Sheriff Nicolson called it the fox corry, 'madadh-ruadh.'

COIR' AN GARBH-CHOIRE. The corry of the rough, or wild corry; a corry within a corry.

COIR' AN LOCHAIN. The little loch corry.

COIR' AN UAIGNEIS. The secret or hidden corry, corry of solitude, sequestered. Sometimes spelled 'Uaigneich' and lies south-east of Blaven.

COIRE BHASADAIR or BASADAIR. The executioner or death-dealer corry. Frequently given, but erroneously, 'Coire Bhaisteir.' Usually spelled 'Coire a'Bhasteir'.

COIRE CHAISE or CHAISEACH. Cheese or cheesy corry. May be so called from some Easter customs or rites. Between Sgurr nan Each and Belig.

COIRE FAOIN. The empty or lonely corry.

COIRE GHREADAIDH, GHREETA, GHRETA, GHRITA. The corry of torment; also found given as 'of the running or flowing water.'

COIRE LAGAN, LABAIN. Various meanings; *La ban*, white or fair day, or dawn; *laban*, mire, dirty place; *lagan*, little hollow or dell.

COIRE NA BANACHDICH or BANACHDAICH. Small pox—or more correctly—vaccination corry. Said to be so named from the pock-marked or pitted surface of the rocks.

COIRE NA CREICHE. The corry of the spoil, where that taken by the Macdonalds from the Macleods after a fierce fight in 1601, was divided.

COIRE NAN LAOGH. The corry of the calves or deer-fawns; on north side of Marsco.

COIRE NAN URAISG, URUISG. The corry of the monsters or hobgoblins, kind of Highland satyrs! Now spelled 'Coir-uisg,' lies above Loch Coruisk.

COIRE ODHAR. The dun or dun-coloured corry.

COIRE RIABHACH. The russet corry. North-east of Sgurr nan Gillean.

COIRE SGREAMHACH, SGREAMHAIL. The loathsome or awful corry. In the Red Hills.

CORUISK, CORUISG, COIRUISGE, COIRUISK (Coir' uisge.) The corry of water, or cauldron.

COOLIN, CUILLIN, CULINN, CUILFHIONN, CUILDHEAN, CUILIONN. Holly. The above are only a few of the different spellings found given for this word. The holly (*Ilex aquafolium*) is from the Anglo-Saxon word *Holeynn*, pronounced hoolynn, not unlike the Scottish Gaelic pronunciation of to-day. Among other erroneous meanings, this name was for long maintained

to have been named after Cuchulain, the noble son of Sualtain. Sheriff Nicolson was a great authority on matters relating to Skye, and he called it A'Chuilionn. The spelling of the Coolins is dealt with at great length in the S.M.C. Guide and should be consulted by all those who are interested.

CORRAN, AN. A point of land reaching out into the sea, sometimes curved like a reaping-hook. This includes in some places a narrow passage through which the tide runs swiftly.

COULLNACRAGGAN, CUIL NA CREAGAN. The recess in or of the rocks.

CREACHAN, AN CREACHANN. The little stack or hill. Generally applicable to the summit of a hill.

CREAG and CREAGAN. Rock, rocks, or little rock.

CREAG AN IOLAIRE. The eagle rock. Nead na h'Iolaire, the eagle's nest; a spur of Sgurr nan Gillean.

CRO. A circle, a sheep fold; also a district surrounded by hills.

CRON. Head of land; perhaps Sròn.

CRUACHAN, AN or NA. The little heap or stack, or the heaps, stacks, pinnacles, haunches, or summits of hills.

CRUACH NA BEINNE. Stack or peak of the mountain, the very top.

CRUAIDH CHOIRE. Hard corry or corrie, thought hard to travel; a small 'bad step' here.

CRUINN BHEINN. Round mountain; a case of the adjective preceding the noun.

CUITHIR. A rocky and cave-studded spot, four miles north of Storr.

CULNAMEAN, CUL NAM BEANN. Back of the mountain. At the north end of Loch Brittle.

DIALLAID, DIOLLAID. Saddle, a ridge to the north of Sgurr nan Gobhar.

DIANAVAIG. shelter, refuge bay, *dion vik.*

DORUS, DORUIS, AN. The door, a pass between Sgurr a'Ghreadaidh and Sgurr a'Mhadaidh said to have been used specially by the Macleods.

DROCHAID. A bridge.

DRUIM. A ridge, in connection with place names.

DRUIM-EADAR-DA-CHOIRE. A ridge between two corries—Coire na Creiche.

DRUIM NA RAMH, RAIMH, NAN RAMH. The ridge of the wood or tree roots. Rises between Coruisk and Harta Corrie.

DRUMHAIN. Ridge of the hinds.

DRYNOCH, DRYNIOCK, DRIOGHNEACH. Place of the thorns.

DUIRINISH. Dere or deer-ness, deer-promontory. One of the four districts in the north of Skye, the others being, Minginish, Trotternish and Vaternish.

DUNAN. The little hill or fort, a hillock.

DUN. A stronghold. There are over fifty duns in Skye.

DUNANS. The little duns. To the south of Flodigarry.

DUNTULM, DUN-TUILM, DUNTOLM. The fort or castle on the round hillock or isolated hill;

numerous spellings. The remains of the ancient seat of the Macdonalds now in ruins.

DUNVEGAN. The variants of this name existing and found in old titles are very numerous. As might be expected, various etymologies have been found, such as, 'Dun Beagan,' the fort of the few, or little fort; 'Dun Viking,' the fort of the viking or sea rover, etc. Dunvegan Castle is situated near the terminus of Loch Fallort, six miles from the main sea; also called Loch Dunvegan.

EAS. A waterfall.

EAS MOR. The great waterfall. It is on the Allt Coire na Banachdich above Glen Brittle Lodge.

EDINBANE, EDINBAIN, EDDIN-BAIN. The fair face or surface, from natural features of the district which has a fine, sunny exposure.

EILEAN, sometimes OILEAN. Island, isle, islet.

ELGOL, ELGOLL, ELGALL, EALAGHOLLA, EALLAGHOLLO, ELLIGHUIL, ELLIGUIL. Noble dale.

EORABUS. Shore farm, a narrow low tongue of land, a narrow ridge of earth and stones, a long sandy promontory, a shore or boundary.

EYNORD, EYNORT, ENARD. Island sea-firth.

EYRE, EYRAR, EYRR, ORE. A gravelly beach, shore or boundary.

FAS. A homestead, residence, a level piece of ground suitable for resting.

FASACH. The desert; also grassy headland of a ploughed field, forest, uncultivated land.

FEADAN, AM. The rock-pipe, water-pipe, small cascade; opening in a wall or even a narrow glen.

FIACAL, FIACAILL A BHASADAIR. The tooth, mountain edge, or peak of the Executioner.

FIACLAN DEARG, FIACLAN FUAR. Red teeth, cold teeth; small boulders on the face of a cliff or precipice of Marsco; these have been named 'Marscoite'; here the estates of Macdonald, Macleod, and Mackinnon once met and converged, and the respective chiefs of these leading clans used to meet there, and drink healths, each standing on his own estate or property.

FIDEAN, NA FIDEIN. The green islets or spots uncovered at high tide.

FIONN CHOIRE. White, fair, or light corry. Between Bruach na Frithe and Sgurr a'Bhasteir.

FIREACH CLACH, CLACHACH. Stony moor.

FLADA, FLADDA, FLADDER, BLADDA, PHLADDA, HADAY. Many other spellings. Flat island.

FLODDA. Float island, or ship island.

FLODIGARRY, FLODGERY. The floating enclosure or place. Very fertile and beautiful. Near Staffin. Pron. *Flo-digary*.

GARADUBH, GARADH DUBH. Black dyke or ridge.

GARBH BHEINN. The rough or wild mountain. North of Blaven.

GARBH CHOIRE. Rough or wild corry, between Sgurr Dubh and Garsbheinn.

GARRAHAN, GEARRDHAN,

GEARRAIDHEAN. Grazing place for cattle.

GARRIE, GARRY. Norse, a farm, generally in terminations.

GARSBHEINN.—mount. Not known. Possibly the echoing mountain. Pron. *Garsven*. Southern terminus of the Main Ridge of the Coolins.

GLAIC AN DUBHAIR. Hollow of the shade or darkness.

GLAIC-GLUMAGACH. The hollow of pools. Near Broadford.

GLAIS BHEALACH. The Green Pass. At Beinn Dearg Mor.

GLAIS-BHEINN NAM FIADH. The green mount of the deer. Near Loch Eynort.

GLAMAIG, GLAMAG. The greedy woman or female. Conical peak opposite Sligachan.

GLAS-BHEINN. Green mount, In Strath.

GLEANN. A glen.

GLEANN BREATAL, BRETILL, GLEN BRITTLE. Meaning not found.

GLUMAIG. The deep pool.

GNOGAN, GNOGANE, GROGAIRE, AN CNOMHAG, CNOMHAGAN, CNOMHAGAG. The large whelk, periwinkle, or buckie.

GRESHERNISH, GRESHORNISH. Grice or pig's ness.

HABOST, HABOIST, THABOST. Sloping farm or homestead, or the dwelling on the slope, high town.

HALIBHAL, HALIVAL, HALLIVAILS, HEALAVAL, HELVELS. The fell with ridge of terraces. Compare Helaval.

HARLOSH. Buck tail. A point on Loch Bracadale.

HARPORT, HERPORT. Goat fiord.

HARTA CORRY or COIRE THARTA, HART-O-CORRY. The corry of the hart, in the Coolins.

HESKEVAL. The fell of the rocky ridge.

HELAVAL, HOLBHAM, HELVEL. Flagstone fell. There are two Helavals with green flat summits, familiarly known as 'Macleods Tables.'

HOLM, HOLME, HOLMS, HOLLOM. The holm, or small island in a bay or river, low-lying land; also an isolated hill.

HORNISCO. The place of eagles.

IASGAIR. The fisher.

IDRIGAL, IDRIGIL, IORIGLE, UADRIGILL. Outer hill, cleft, or gully.

INBHIR, AN IONBHAR. The confluence with the sea. An estuary.

INIS, INNIS. An island; it is now obsolete and has been replaced by *eilean*.

KILBRIDE, KILBRIDYE, KILBRY. Saint Bridget's cell or church.

KILMUIR. St. Mary's cell or church, formerly named or called Kilmaluag.

KINGSBURGH, KINGSBURROW, KISBURGH, etc. Toll-town.

KIRKABOST, KIRKIBOST. Church-place at the home farm or town.

KYLEAKIN, KEILLAKIN. Acunn's strait or kyle. (?) Hakon.

LAGAN, LAGGAN. Little hollow.

LAPLACH, LAPACH, LABACH. A swampy or boggy place.

LEAC. A ledge of rock jutting out from the foot or base of a cliff on the foreshore and covered by the sea at flood-tide.

LEACANN. The broad side of a hill, a broad slope, steep shelving ground, also a steep green surface.

LEACACH. Having sheets of rock piled flat over each other.

LEATHAD. A slope or declivity.

LEITIR, LEITER, AN LETH TIR. A sloping hill on one side, and glen or plain, half the land cut away.

LIAN. A meadow.

LOCH, LAKE. Arm of the sea. According to Celtic custom the inland lochs are named after the stream that flows through or from the same, the stream being the primary cause of their existence, consequently the older.

LOCH AN FHIR BHALLAICH, LOCHAN. Loch or little loch of the spotted or marked man (pock-marked)? Just below Coire Lagan.

LOCH NA H-AIRDE. Little loch of the aird, height, or promontory. At Rudh'an Dunain.

LOCH FADD, FAD, FADA, LOCHA-FADA. The long loch or lochs. Below Storr and Quiraing.

LOCH HASCO. The loch of the high place. Below Quiraing, has no outlet, and is very deep and clear.

LOCH LANGAIG. Long-bay loch. Below Leac na Fionn.

LOCH LEATHANN. The broad loch; below Storr and famed for its trout.

LOCH SLAPIN, SLEIPPAN, SLAOPAIN. The sluggish, muddy loch.

LOCH SLIGACHAN. Loch of the shells, or shelly land or place.

LÓN. A wet meadow or marsh.

LOTA COIRE. Loft corry. A continuation of Harta Corry.

LUIB. The bend or corner or little glen.

MAM, MAAM. Rounded hill.

MACLEOD'S MAIDENS. The name given in English to certain up-standing rocks in the sea, south of Duirinish, near Idrigil. Macleod's Tables are to the north.

MARSCO, MARSCOW. Sea-gull rock. The pyramidal mountain in Glen Sligachan.

MEALL. A heap or almost shapeless hill.

MEALL NA CUILCE. Hillock of the reeds, near Coruisk.

MEALL NA SUIREANACH. The hillock, height, or table of the maiden or nymph.

MINGINISH. There are some thirty different spellings. The great promontory.

MOL, MOLL, MAL, MUL. Shingly or pebbly beach.

PABBA, PABBAY, PAPA. Father (monk or priest) island.

PORT NAN LONG. The port or harbour of the ships. Famous Skye tweed made here. Near Loch Harport.

PORTREE, PORTROI, PORTRY. The king's port or harbour. The Metropolis of Skye.

QUIRAING, CUIRAING. The round fold or pen; also given as the recess or pit of the row or range of rock pillars. Undoubtedly the most marvellous rock scenery in all Britain. Near the northern tip of Skye.

RAASAY. Roe-isle or roe-ridge-isle. Opposite Portree.

RHUDUNAN, RHUEDUNAN, RUDH-AN-UNAIN. The point or promontory at the little hill.

ROMASDAL, ROMASDAIL, ROMISDALE. Giant or giant's dale.

RONA. Rough or rocky isle.

RUADH STAC. Red stack; case of adjective preceding noun, and intensifying meaning, a stack of redness.

RUAMAN, RUDH' AMAN. River point or promontory.

RUDHA, RUGHA, RUTHA. A point or promontory.

RUDH' AN DUNAN, DUNAIN. Dunan, or the little hill, point. In Soay Sound. There is a dun or fort here in ruins.

RUDHA NA H-AIRDE. Point of the height.

RUDHA NA H-AIRDE GLAISE. Point of the grey or green point. North of Portree.

RUIGHE, RIGHE. Outstretched base of a mountain, a sheiling.

SCALPA, SCALPAY, SGALPA, SKALPA. Cave island.

SCAVAIG, SGATHVAIG, SGATHAVAIG. The shadowy, gloomy, or dark bay in the loch of the same name.

SCONSAR, SCOUSAR. Not known.

SCORE, SCOIR, SCOR, SGOR. The peak, also a township in Kilmuir.

SCORRIBREAC, SCORRIBREAK. The speckled, or parti-coloured rock.

SCOURIE. Place of birds.

SGEIR. An isolated rock which barely disappears under water, and with no vegetation.

SGIATH. Wing, piece of land jutting into the sea; also sheltered side of a mountain or district.

SGUMAN, AN. The stack or stack-shaped hill. Generally spelled Sgumain.

SGURR. A large steep rock or precipice; numerous spellings—scoor, scor, scorr, scour, scuir, scur, sgoar, sgor, sgorr.

SGURR, A'BHASTEIR, BHAISTEIR, BHASADAIR. The peak of the executioner.

SGURR A'CHOIRE BHIG. Peak of the little corry. Pron. *Vick*.

SGURR A'FIONN-CHOIRE. Peak of the white or bright corry, or cold corry.

SGURR A'GHREADAIDH. Pron. *greeta*. Peak of torment, anxiety, thrashings, mighty winds.

SGURR ALASDAIR. Alexander's peak. Highest in the Coolins and named after Alexander Nicolson who was the first to climb it in 1873.

SGURR A'MHADAIDH. Pron. *Vatee*, the foxes' peak. Actually there are four separate tops.

SGURRAN, AN. The little peak; thought may be Sgurr a'Fionn-Choire.

SGURR AN FHEADAIN, SGURR NA FEADAIN. Pron. *Aityan*, peak of the water-pipe.

SGURR COIR' AN LOCHAIN. Peak of the corry of the loch. Forms a lower buttress of Sgurr Thearlaich.

SGURR DEARG. Pron. *Jerrack*, the red peak. Actual summit is the top of the Inaccessible Pinnacle.

A spur of this peak on the Main Ridge is An Stac, the stack.

SGURR DUBH AN DA-BHEINN. The black peak of the double mountain, perhaps the peak at the junction of two ridges. Pron. *Sgurr Doo na Da Ven*.

SGURR EADAR-DA-CHOIRE. The peak between two corries.

SGURR LAGAN, LAGHAIN. Old name for Sgurr Alasdair.

SGURR MHIC COINNICH. Mackenzie's Peak; named after a famous guide to the Coolins.

SGURR NA BANACHDICH, A BHANACHDAICH. Small-pox peak; so called after the peculiar rock formation of its corry. Known locally as Sgurr na Banachaig, the dairymaids' peak.

SGURR NA BHAIRNICH. Peak of the limpet.

SGURR NA H-EIDHNE. Ivy peak.

SGURR NA H'UAMHA. Cave peak; the northern terminus of the Main Ridge of the Coolins. Pron. *Sgurr na Hoo-a*.

SGURR NAN EACH. Horses' peak. North of Blaven.

SGURR NAN EAG. The notched or serrated peak.

SGURR NAN GILLEAN, SGOR-GILLEAN. The lads' peak, peak of the young men, gillies, servants or gylls. The most shapely mountain in the Coolins.

SGURR NAN GOBHAR. Goats' peak.

SGURR NA STRI, STRITH. Peak of the conflict or fight—opposing winds.

SGURR SGUMAIN. *See* An Sguman.

SGURR THEARLAICH, SGURR-

TEARLACH. Charles' Peak; named after Charles Pilkington and formerly known as northeast peak (of Alasdair).

SGURR THORMAID. Norman's peak, named after the late Norman Collie.

SGURR THUILM. Pron. *Hulim*, peak of Tulm.

SKEABOST, SKAEBOST, SGEUBOST, SGAITHBOST. The sheltered house.

SKYE, SKY. *An t-Eilean-Sgitheanach*, 'the sky.' The familiar name, used by the natives especially, is *Eilean-a-Cheo*, the isle of mist, or *An t-Eilean*, the island.

SLEAT. The mountain slopes, or sloping moorland. Numerous spellings.

SLIGACHAN, SLIGICHAN, SLEIGACHAN, SLIGEACHAN, SLIGNEACHAN. The shelly place.

SNIZORT, SNISORT, SNESFURD. Snow fiord.

SOAY, SOA, SOADH, SOYEA. The isle of swine.

SRON NA CREITHEACH. The promontory of the brushwood, poplar or aspen; it is another name for Camasunary valley, Creithreach meaning a clayey place, a bog.

SRON VOURLINN, STRONVEULIN. The mill point or promontory. Near Flodigarry.

STAC, AN. The stack or rock. Compare Sgurr Dearg.

STAFFIN, STAFAIN, STAFIN, STAPHAIN. The place of staff-like

or upright pillars. The seaboard here abounds in basaltic and other columnar and pillared rocks.

STORR, STOR. The steep high cliff or pinnacle.

STRATH. The low-lying, level land between hills.

STRATH NA CREITHEACH. The boggy valley, near Camasunary.

STRATHAIRD, AIRD-AN-T-SRATH. The height of Strath.

STRUAN, SRUTHAN. The streamlet.

SUIDHE. A seat.

TAIRNEILEAR. The thunderer. A part of Coire na Creiche.

TALISKER, TALASCAIR, TALLASKARR, THALASGAIR. The house of or at the rock.

TOBAR. A well.

TOR, TORR. A pointed hill or tower-like rock.

TORRAN, NA TORRAIN, TORRIN. The heaps, mounds or tumuli.

TORVAIG, TORAIG. Hill bay.

TROTTERNISH, TROTERNISH, TROTERNESS, TRONTERNESS, TROUTERNESS. Thrond's headland or point. The most northerly district in Skye.

TULLOCH, TULLOCH GORM. The hillock, the green hillock.

TULM, TOLM AN T-HOLM. The stack or cliff.

UAMH, UAMHA. The cave.

UIDH. The ford.

UIG, UIGE, WIG, VIG. The nook, or retired place.

VATERNISH, VADIRNES. The water point or promontory. A north-western district of Skye.

On the present occasion I travelled to Skye at the beginning of May and during the preceding winter months had often imagined myself sailing past its windy headlands and entering Portree harbour on a lovely evening with an azure sky, fleeting cumulus clouds, and a glittering sea rippling away in the sunlight to the four corners of its land-locked bay.

This dream, however, never came true because on arriving at the Kyle of Lochalsh from Euston I found no steamers sailing and was greeted by rain and mist instead of sunshine. My coming to the Misty Isle thus lost much of its romance and instead was just prosaic, for I took one of the many buses that serve its remote corners and stepped off it at Sligachan instead of going on to Portree. I spent the first few days in walking vast distances to get myself in training for the strenuous days ahead, and then motored over the moors to Portree where I put up at the Royal Hotel.

Portree occupies one of the most beautiful situations in Skye. A crescent of white cottages sweep round the harbour, still more houses rise above them in the trees (3), and a street of shops leads to a large square which is the changing point for the buses that radiate to the far-flung places of the island. On the outskirts of the town are the more pretentious dwellings and beyond them the engirdling moorland, dominated by Fingal's Seat and shutting out the view to the west. The pier juts out into the sea at the end of the harbour (2), and above it rises a wooded hill dominated by a tower now lying in ruins. The bay presents an enchanting picture with its boats bobbing up and down on the restless sea; it is hemmed in by precipitous cliffs and shapely hills with Raasay lying across the channel (5), the peaks of Torridon forming a serrated skyline in the background. Ben Tianavaig frowns upon this lovely seascape and rises to the south-east with a pointed top (1,352 feet (412 m)) (4). Its basaltic cliffs stand out in the evening light against its vast sweeps of green pasturage, and opposite it on the north side of the sound, but out of sight of the town, rise a long line of magnificent headlands, of which Rudha

Plate 2 Portree Harbour

na h'Airde Glaise is the most conspicuous with its crest 1,000 feet (305 m) above the ocean (9).

I spent a happy day exploring the environs of Portree. The place appeared to be deserted save for the occasional shopper who no sooner seemed to arrive from the country to make his purchases than he disappeared again to his abode in the hills. I think the pleasantest walk was by the tree-girt path that meanders round the northern shores of the bay. You have before you the scene I have already described, but when you take the first bend in the coastline you see far away to the south, in the dip beyond the shallow reaches of Portree Loch, the jagged outline of the Coolins with the great mass of Glamaig on their left (6). You stroll along the leafy path, revelling in the glorious tang of the breeze, and in the ceaseless murmur of the sea which beats upon the maze of black boulders strewn everywhere. Ahead of you across the channel Ben Tianavaig now seems so near that you can clearly perceive the innumerable caves riddling its sea edge, but it is the surprise view disclosed as you round the point that makes this walk worth while, for the long green slopes of the headlands, capped with lofty cliffs, afford a typical picture of this fine coast (9).

Apart from the inherent charms of the place, Portree is a splendid centre for the motorist and the two most popular tours take in many of the interesting places. You may follow the great north road to Kingsburgh and Uig, and then continue northwards to Duntulm, returning by Staffin and the Storr. If you prefer to take a nearer view of the Coolins, and of the marvellous seaboard of some of the western lochs, you will go south from Portree to Sligachan, turn right for Loch Bracadale observing the slender columns of MacLeod's Maidens off Idrigill Point, and then go on to view the modernised Castle of Dunvegan where so many fascinating relics of its past glory are shown to the visitor, returning by the road which skirts the narrow arms of Loch Snizort before again reaching Portree.

Plate 4 Ben Tianavaig from Portree Bay

Plate 5 The narrow entrance to Portree Bay

Plate 6 Glamaig and the Coolins from Portree Bay

Plate 7 The Kilt Rock

This road climbs out of Portree and for much of its way runs along a moorland shelf which separates the spectacular backbone of Trotternish from the high cliffs frowning upon the Sound of Raasay, and further north reveals an uninterrupted prospect of the peaks in the northern counties of the mainland. The long mountain ridge, so well seen from this road, is worthy of notice because of the magnificence of its precipitous riven face, basaltic terraces, and weird pinnacles, which at its southern end overhang the road, and after tailing away across the moorland are again approached so closely at its northern extremity.

Sheriff Nicolson first made its traverse famous as one of the grandest walks in Skye, but whether he actually negotiated the whole of it is a matter of conjecture, since from Beinn a'Chearcaill in the south to Sgurr Mor in the north is a good twenty miles (34 km) if the twists of the ridge are kept to. Moreover, the undulations of its crests are not inconsiderable, for the average height is perhaps 2,000 feet (610 m) with many drops in between the conspicuous summits of Storr, Baca Ruadh, Beinn Edra and Meall na Suiramach. The views from the ridge are spacious and entrancing, for on the east the peaks of Applecross and Torridon are well seen beyond the island chain of Raasay and South Rona, and on the west the moorland slopes down disclosing Loch Bracadale and the heights of Healaval Beg and More, known more familiarly as MacLeod's Tables, with their strangely flattened tops, together with the rugged coastline of Vaternish across the great expanse of Loch Snizort. To the north the dim blue hills of the Outer Hebrides rise from the sea to stretch right across the skyline, whilst in the south are the splintered peaks of the ever-present Coolins.

The Staffin Road is not good, but by the time this book appears it may have been improved sufficiently to make the journey over it more comfortable. You leave behind the last cottages of Portree which from their elevated position command such lovely views across the bay. The road twists and turns as it mounts beside the River Chracaig and then straightens out on

Plate 8 The Storr from Loch Fada

reaching the vast expanse of rolling moorland. When you attain its highest point at about 600 feet (183 m), Loch Fada is suddenly revealed in the basin below together with the great frowning bastions of the Storr, whose Old Man appears as a strange, isolated pinnacle on their right (8). The road drops downhill and passes the remote cottage situated on the shore of the loch which is a favourite with trout fishermen. Before you have left it behind you are running beside Loch Leathan with the savage precipices of the Storr soaring overhead.

The road now runs nearer the sea and after rounding many a swelling in the moorland you cross the bridge spanning the deep ravine whose waterfalls are worthy of notice. On and on you go, with a changing scene at every turn in the road, until you pull up at Loch Mealt which lies almost on the verge of the great sea cliffs. Here you will walk a few yards to a sensational overhang on their crest, which not only discloses the magnificent ribbed Kilt Rock whose columns resemble the basaltic pillars of Staffa, but also the waterfall issuing from the face of the cliffs to fall in fine spray on the boulder strewn shore far below (7). Continuing northwards again you will soon perceive more signs of life, for the lonely habitations of the crofters (11) give place to the more substantially built houses of Staffin. These are dotted about amid the cultivated fields that fringe the sweeping shore of the bay and through the channel which separates Staffin Island from the point of An Corran you may pick out the isolated peak of Slioch from the galaxy of mountains on the mainland (10).

The road forks at Staffin; the left branch following a westerly course to pass over a low gap in the ridge and eventually to rejoin the main road again at Uig on the shore of Loch Snizort; the right branch going northwards past many a wee lochan at the base of the grotesque pinnacles of Quiraing, and after threading the hillocks of Dunans, bringing you finally to Flodigarry. Here you will discover Flora Macdonald's Cottage (14) situated behind the hotel (12) whose superb situation overlooks the Minch and Staffin Bay (13) and provides enchanting prospects in all directions.

Plate 9 Rudha na h'Airde Glaise

Plate 10 Staffin Bay

Plate 11 A crofter's cottage at Dunans

Plate 12 Sron Vourlinn from the Flodigarry Hotel

Plate 13 Staffin Bay from Flodigaryy

Plate 14 Flora Macdonald's home at Flodigarry

Those who motor from Kyleakin to Portree will see the Storr for the first time as they skirt the northern slopes of the peninsula between Loch Ainort and Loch Sligachan. If the day is clear they will easily perceive its fantastic buttresses topping the Trotternish skyline and merging with the sea at Rudha nam Brathairean.

Before commencing the present journey, I had read all the descriptions of the Storr I could find but had searched in vain for photographs that would give me a clearer conception of its topography. Beyond the rather ubiquitous picture of the Old Man (15), however, I was unable to discover anything of interest so that when I came to explore it I was amazed at its impressive and grotesque character. I took a taxi from Portree to Loch Leathan (16), and the Scot who drove me, although a native of Skye, admitted he had never been nearer to it than the road and when he left me I believe he never expected to see me again!

I walked over the green slopes extending upwards from Loch Leathan for perhaps a mile, and when the ground steepened I took to a shallow gully which opens out below the gigantic buttress on the left of the main group. Skirting its base I soon encountered the 'Guardians of the Sanctuary' whose shattered pinnacles and castellated tors soared into the thinly curtaining cirrus of the sky (17). On entering the enclosed basin behind them I obtained my first close view of the terraced central buttress which is the most prominent of them all and rises overhead almost vertically, its sides tapering to a rough narrow crest (18).

I wended my way to the right over the piles of scree, and in and out of the astonishingly varied collection of rocks, all of which were riven by frost, wind and rain, and had stood there for centuries in a gradual state of decay. Here indeed was one of Nature's wild workshops, a barren wilderness of stone, surrounded on one side by precipitous cliffs deeply cut by gullies, and on the other by every conceivable variety of ghostly pinnacle pointing upwards to an empty sky and hiding the wonderfully contrasting beauty which, below this Sanctuary, stretched to the far horizon in every direction. I was so amazed at the weirdness of this display that I stood there in the brooding silence and imagined myself transported back through the ages to the Celtic era, with the fabulous creatures of their mythology lurking at every corner and their priests waiting to initiate some ghastly human sacrifice.

Turning away from this desolation I crossed a low ridge to get a closer view of the Old Man and his satellites which now appeared more imposing than when seen from the road below (20). Later on I climbed up to examine this leaning obelisk of trap rock which is 160 feet (49 m) high and undercut at its base, but before doing so I ascended high ground nearby to compare it with the long line of cliffs behind (21). Finally, I wandered over to the most northerly point to get a better conception of it as a whole and then scrambled up the lowest of the broken buttresses to see the marvellous panorama.

I lingered long over this delightful scene, and then, picking up my rucksack and cameras, commenced the traverse of the immense buttresses, keeping close to their edges all the time as I climbed them one after the other. The gullies presented a sensational aspect from above, with their sheer broken walls often framing the Old Man hundreds of feet below at their base. This part of the Storr circuit was the most exhilarating because it afforded so many varied aspects of the whole scene and from such airy viewpoints too; but I think the finest prospect was revealed as I turned to walk along the crest of the most southerly buttress since it displayed the vastness of the great precipices frowning upon the diminutive Old Man and his satellites below (22). The view from the lower end of this sloping buttress was not so good (23), but it provided an interesting comparison with that from the northern extremity of the Sanctuary (24). I continued my walk along the crest of the cliffs and found a narrow gully threaded by a tinkling burn, and to its merry music I descended over a carpet of primroses, violets and daisies to the open moorland. I reached the road in the late afternoon, and trudged its six miles (10 km) to Portree well satisfied with the joys of this wonderful day.

Plate 15 The Old Man of Storr

Plate 16 The Storr from Loch Leathan

Plate 17 The Guardians of the Sanctuary

Plate 18 The Central Buttress

Plate 19 The Needle Rock

Plate 21 The Northern Buttress from the Old Man

Plate 22 The frowning precipices of Storr with the Old Man below

Plate 24 The Sanctuary from the North

Plate 25 The Tooth

Before embarking upon the present journey I knew nothing of
Leac na'Fionn; I had seen no reference to it in the literature, nor
had I noticed it on the map; yet, it was the first thing that caught
my eye on going to Flodigarry and I was immediately imbued
with a desire to explore it. The weather broke down as soon as I
arrived at this romantically situated hotel, and my reason for
staying there was not only to enjoy the marvellous seascape for
which it is famous, but more especially to be near Quiraing so
that I could climb it at the first favourable opportunity.

What appealed to me about Leac na'Fionn was that it
appeared to be an isolated tableland whose ramparts seemed
unscaleable, and whether I looked at it from Loch Langaig (26),
or from any of the nearby heights (27), I could discover no
weakness in its defences. This intrigued me so much that on the
first fine afternoon I set out to solve this problem and if the
weather held I proposed afterwards to go on to Quiraing which
rises on its left and is perhaps a mile to the south (27). I walked
down the high road to Loch Langaig and followed the well-
marked cart track which passes over into the little glen behind it,
but leads only to a peat bed. Crossing the intervening hillocks, all
covered thickly with deep heather and bent, I mounted the steep
ground rising to Leac na'Fionn, but went off to the right when
half way up the slope to examine the Tooth only clearly seen
from immediately below (25).

I then climbed up to the base of the precipitous cliffs, but
finding no break in them, walked round their flanks for a
considerable distance. As with all our British mountains, there is
usually an easy way to the summit, and this great hill proved to
be no exception to this rule, for on passing the base of the third
buttress I discovered a steep grassy gully completely separating it
from the fourth and last buttress of them all. The angle of the
slippery grass was such that I could touch its sides and I found
the easiest way to ascend it was by zig-zagging from one edge to
the other. Up and up I went, penetrating more deeply into the
great face of rock with every step, until a few feet of scree finally

placed me on its top. Imagine my surprise, however, when I discovered its narrow crest merely joined the two islands of rock, and dropped down immediately on the other side as a long scree shoot to the hidden glen beneath. Looking back from the crest of the fourth buttress revealed the almost vertical profile of the other three with their cliffs facing the east and with the coastline of the island below (28). The western face, however, though sheer, was terraced, but this was not continuous and the rock seemed to be loose and rotten so that it offered little scope for the rock-climber (29). The top of the fourth buttress was of naked rock but the other three formed one level stretch covered with grass that would have made an excellent bowling green! The whole platform seemed to be poised in the sky and afforded an excellent vantage point for the appraisal of the panorama in all directions. The view through the exit of the gully was striking and its walls framed perfectly the two small islands off Flodigarry, but the haze that hung over the sea hid the peaks of Torridon away to the east (30). While I rested, the weather changed again and a storm appeared to be blowing up from the south-west. This lent a grim aspect to the pinnacles of Quiraing across the great gap, but a ray of weak sunlight illuminated the gully which usually forms the approach to the Table from Flodigarry. Beyond it the long ridge stretched away southwards to end with the prominent summit of the Storr (31).

Continuing my exploration, I climbed down the western face of Leac na'Fionn and then made my way to the right over tumbled scree to the head of the little glen where I found another tiny lochan nestling at the base of the Redoubt (32). A low ridge cut the glen into two halves longitudinally and I walked along it to its southern extremity where I found another great Tooth which caught the last gleam of sunlight before the approaching storm (33).

It was now late afternoon and I should have taken the wiser course of hurrying back to my hotel before the storm broke, but I foolishly scrambled up to the famous Table of Quiraing and had just reached it when the heavens burst and drenched me to the skin.

Plate 26 Leac na' Fionn from Loch Langaig

Plate 28 The Eastern Buttress

Plate 29 The Western Buttress

Plate 30 The islands of Flodigarry

Plate 31 The Trotternish Ridge and Quiraing

Plate 32 The Redoubt

Plate 33 The storm approaches the Southern Tooth

Quiraing

The weird rocks of Quiraing make the most bizarre landscape in Britain. The best distant view of them is obtained from the Staffin Road which passes over to Uig at the low break in the great Trotternish ridge, but the shortest approach from Flodigarry is by taking a direct line over the moors.

On two occasions I ascended to the Table which is secretly hidden up amid the gaunt, grotesque pinnacles of Quiraing. The first time I got wet to the skin and saw nothing of its amazing rock architecture, but nevertheless witnessed one of those demonstrations of the 'Wrath of the Gods' when all the elements combine to transform a masterpiece of Nature into a wild cauldron of the Devil. The second time I started off on a dull day when everything was steeped in gloom, but the fresh north-west wind that sprang up in the early afternoon brought sailing white clouds, a blue sky and brilliant sunlight.

On the present occasion, I followed the highway to Staffin and turned off to the right along the rough mountain road to Uig, but deserted it about a mile (1·69 km) below the pass. Striking out across the moor I took a direct line for the beetling cliffs, which prelude the approach to Quiraing's inner sanctuary, and thus obtained a comprehensive idea of its topography together with that of the Prison whose overhanging walls face the Needle (35).

Scrambling up to a rough ridge running parallel with the buttresses but at some distance away from them, I halted to examine these gigantic, terraced precipices (34), and whilst standing there a fall of rock occurred on my left, several large boulders crashing down the side of the cliffs and throwing up clouds of dust to the consternation of some sheep feeding on the patches of sparse grass nearby. I continued along the crest of the ridge, which finally merges with the Prison, and after scaling its overhanging crags to reach its summit, discovered I could have avoided them by a steep grass slope on the other side (36). This coign of vantage disclosed a fine view of the shattered pinnacles and bastions of Quiraing (37).

Descending from the Prison, I picked up the well-marked track which zig-zags up the scree, and when abreast of the Needle Rock, climbed to a ledge on the left hand wall of the buttress to obtain a better view of it (39). This obelisk is about 120 feet (37 m) high and overhangs considerably as may be seen by looking down on it from above (38). The innumerable pinnacles of all sizes and shapes which flank this gully provided an awesome spectacle as I climbed. Eventually I emerged from this wild ravine to set foot upon the grassy undulating corridor which encircles the Table. Here a great frowning pinnacle soars into the sky as the last grim guardian of the secret entrance to the sanctuary (41).

I did not immediately ascend to the Table in front of me, but bearing to the left climbed to the top of the great buttress so that I could the more easily obtain a comprehensive view of the whole scene (42). The southern end of the Table is perhaps 30 or 40 feet (9 m or 12 m) above the grassy corridor but its northern extremity merges with the engirdling mural precipices of Meall na Suiramach (43). I walked round to see it from the other end and then measured its level grassy top which I found to be 100 paces long by 50 paces wide. It would have made a grand Putting Green with its slight undulations, but what a fantastic situation for such a game! To the east of it, erosion has worn away the high rock wall which now rises into the sky as two gigantic pinnacles with a tiny one between them and this opening afforded a refreshing glimpse of the sea below (40). The southern end of the enclosure is, however, more open and reveals a vast expanse of moorland with the light glinting on a lochan here and there, and with the sea, the inner isles, and the mainland, beyond (44).

I lingered here for some time while the wind sobbed in the gullies and the great cloud galleons passed overhead in rapid succession. My solitude was undisturbed by the presence of any other human being, but strangely enough two rams were feeding in the grassy hollow.

Ultimately I left it all behind, and descending the scree of the wide gully on the east, crossed the billowy moorland finally to reach my hotel (45).

Plate 34 I scan the gigantic precipices

Plate 35 Quiraing with the Prison on the right

Plate 36 The Prison

Plate 37 Quiraing from the Prison

Plate 38 The Needle and the Prison from above

Plate 39 The Needle Rock

Plate 40 Large and small pinnacles surround the Table

Plate 41 Grim guardians of the mystic Sanctuary

Plate 42 The Table from the South

Plate 43 The Table from the North

Plate 45 Cloud over Quiraing seen from Flodigarry

One afternoon while staying at Flodigarry I went to Duntulm, situated about four miles (7 km) away on the other side of Trotternish. The ruins of the Castle stand on a promontory with a small bay to the east (50), and on the west the waters of the Minch stretch away to the purple hills of Harris lying in an unbroken line on the horizon (52). A narrow neck of land, occupied by a farm, separates it from the road but little of its past glory remains to tell the tale of its former grandeur. The most conspicuous features are two isolated columns, the last remnants of the ancient keep (48 and 49); the gables of what might have been a chapel, standing above a dark vault, on the edge of the cliffs (51); and the remains of a wall whose windows overlook Duntulm Bay and its hummocky island (52).

Duntulm Castle was for centuries the chief seat of the Macdonalds of the Isles and its position must have been the strongest in Skye, for it was unapproachable from the sea (47) and scarcely less so from the land, where it was protected by outlying walls and again by ditches. It was the home of the chief until late in the eighteenth century, and then, unlike the Dunvegan of the MacLeods, it was deserted and left to moulder and decay. According to tradition it was the scene of many dark and gruesome deeds during its occupation, among which that perpetrated by Donald Gorme, its chief, upon Hugh Macghilleasbuig his treacherous kinsman, may be cited here as typical. Hugh plotted against Donald the grim, but was captured by him and brought to Duntulm. There he was placed in the dungeon and slowly starved, salt meat being lowered to him to aggravate this torture which was soon replaced by a raging thirst. Hugh was refused water and suffered great agonies before he died.

Another incident which has passed through the pages of history concerns Donald's wife who was a sister of Rory Mor MacLeod, Lord of Dunvegan. When he fell in love with a daughter of Mackenzie of Kintail, he resolved to be rid of his lawful wife who had unfortunately lost an eye. He turned her out of Duntulm mounted on a one-eyed horse, led by a one-eyed boy, and followed by a one-eyed dog! When this sorry cavalcade arrived at Dunvegan the insult to the MacLeods was revenged by Rory Mor who carried fire and sword throughout Trotternish which resulted in the death of many a Macdonald, the feud being carried on for years by each invading the other's territories in the Outer Hebrides.

Plate 47 The castle from the West

Plate 48 A remnant of the keep

Plate 49 The ancient keep

Plate 50 Duntulm from the East

Plate 51 A gable of the old chapel

Plate 52 Duntulm Bay from the castle

Glen Brittle lies to the west of the Coolins and its few habitations stand at the foot of the long shoulder of Sgurr Dearg. The largest of them is Glen Brittle House, a one-time shooting lodge of the MacLeods, which, together with a number of cottages, housed the invading mountaineer.* The glen is remote and is reached by a rough hill road which leaves the highway to the east of Carbost. After winding its way over the moors to a height of 646 feet (197 m), it descends in sweeping curves through the long green valley, bordered on the west by a band of conifers planted by the Forestry Commission, and soon after passing the conspicuous Youth Hostel at the base of Sgurr nan Gobhar, ends at the Lodge which farms much of its more fertile stretches. The River Brittle drains this vast catchment area and is fed by innumerable burns coming down from the corries. As an increasingly widening stream it finally enters Loch Brittle whose arm penetrates inland about three miles (5 km). The journey from Carbost is full of interest because as the road swings down Glen Brittle it reveals many of the wild western corries and also gives a vivid impression of the great lateral ridges of the Coolins which thrust out their shoulders well into the valley. Those coming by car follow this bumpy road, whereas sturdy wayfarers who step off the bus at Sligachan have to walk the eight miles (14 km) along the track over the Bealach a'Mhaim, which before joining the road affords good views.

Glen Brittle Lodge is surrounded by trees which in spring and summer soften the otherwise barren landscape (55). On the eastern side its windows look out on the peaks of the Coolins (53), which at sunrise make a fretted skyline high above the dark valley. As the sun climbs up behind them the shadows of the peaks themselves may be seen by those occupying the western bedrooms to sink gradually down the heathery flanks of the hills opposite until the whole glen is flooded with the light of day. At

*Glen Brittle House no longer takes guests, but climbers may stay at the BMC Memorial Hut nearby or at the Campsite near Loch Brittle.

eventide this natural phenomenon is reversed, for the sun then falls behind the hills whose shadow creeps slowly up the glowing pink flanks of the Coolins until their tops are finally silhouetted against the starry sky.

The Allt Coir na Banachdich flows down past the garden boundary of the Lodge and in the early morning its playful music may be heard by those who are awake to see the sunrise in the stillness of the glen. From the bridge this burn makes a charming picture, its north bank enlivened in the spring by the bright yellow blossom of the gorse, and its south side flanked by the soft pinkish shoots of the larch. Sgurr Alasdair rises in the background to dominate the scene, and with its satellite Sgumain, is framed between the trees (54).

On the present occasion I was welcomed at Glen Brittle Lodge by Miss Macrae; her genial smile and cheerful disposition reflecting the charm of her late mother, whose kindness still lingers in the memory of legions of mountaineers. It was too early in the season for the house to be full of visitors and I learned that the other three guests were out on the hills and that a further six were expected in the course of the next few days. The afternoon of my arrival was sunny and although it was too late in the day to start on a long expedition, I wandered up the track, and climbing the slopes of Sgurr Dearg, ultimately arrived at the cairn on the Sron. The sun had disappeared while I ascended this ridge and as the mist swept over Sgurr Dearg I dimly perceived the forms of two climbers descending the narrow *arête*, and when they reached me I was delighted to find they were Anthony M. Robinson and his wife whom I had met on a previous occasion at a meeting of the Midland Association of Mountaineers. We completed the descent together and, soon after reaching the Lodge, were joined by Cyril B. Machin, another member of this well-known club and a doughty climber. Rain set in on the morrow and as it was their last day in the south Coolins the former packed ready for their departure whilst the latter went out to brave the elements and traverse the four peaks of Sgurr a'Mhadaidh. Next day they left me and while the rain poured down in torrents I passed the time by looking through the

Plate 54 Alasdair and Sgumain from the Banachdich Burn

Climbers' Book with its many curious entries, and by scanning
the Visitors' Book which is always an interesting occupation.
Here I discovered many friendly names which I give below
because, if perchance they read this book, it may remind them
realistically of happy days on these hills.

Mary L. Abraham.	E. W. Hodge.	F. A. Pullinger.
W. E. Ball.	Robin A. Hodgkin.	N. Ridyard.
Geoffrey Barratt.	H. M. Kelly.	Brenda Ritchie.
Bentley Beetham.	The late H. E. Kretschmer.	The late G. R. Speaker.
Una Cameron.	G. D. Langlands.	Tom Stephenson.
J. Lawson Cook.	G. Graham Macphee.	C. G. Wickham.
W. Heaton Cooper.	C. Douglas Milner.	Graham Wilson.
M. R. FitzGibbon.	Ronald T. Mustchin.	J. E. B. Wright.
Mary D. G. Glynne.	John Poucher (my son).	

In the past 15 years most of these names appeared only once
and a few, twice, but Wright held the record with eight entries,
while Hodge had five, Stephenson four, and Macphee three.

On the next evening, two of the Good Companions arrived.
They were Mr. and Mrs. J. O. Fenwick who were on their
honeymoon and during the succeeding heavenly days we made
some splendid expeditions together. On the following day the
remaining four of the Good Companions reached Glen Brittle
from the south and our party now included C. R. Atkinson and
J. Cook, both of Langdale, and Arthur Robinson and A. S.
Taylor from the not far distant town of Preston.

Conditions improved with the arrival of Arthur Robinson who
in all six of his previous visits to Skye had never experienced bad
weather. The rain ceased and the sun shone so that we were all
able to enjoy several magificent days on the peaks and ridges, of
which the long evenings on the Cioch and in Coire Lagan
together with a traverse of Sgurr a'Ghreadaidh were perhaps the
most enchanting. On some of the evenings we were also
privileged to watch and wait while the shadows crept skywards
on the Coolins, and since Robinson and I had tastes in common
we revelled in the subtleness of colouring as the pink glow on
Sgurr Dearg faded little by little until its wan face told of the
setting of the sun away to the west.

Plate 55 Alasdair, Sgumain and Sron na Ciche from Glen Brittle

I have elsewhere described the fascination of *Coire Lagan* so there is no need for me to refer to it in detail again here (58), and although I have written of Sron na Ciche in a later section it may be of interest to mention that its grand face of rock extends for about one mile (1·69 km) and is perhaps the happiest hunting ground of the rock climber in the whole of the Coolins (57).

Coire a'Ghrunnda displays the largest expanse of boiler plates in the western Coolins so that all who come to Glen Brittle should make a point of going there to see it (59). As I have said elsewhere difficulties will be encountered by those who follow the course of the stream and it is safer to ascend on the left where a nice scramble leads to the lonely lochan lying in its vast basin. While this closer view of the enormous slabs of Alasdair is of interest (60), the proximity of this peak considerably foreshortens its real majesty which is seen to best advantage from Sgurr nan Eag (85).

Coire na Banachdich is so near to Glen Brittle that its exploration may be undertaken on an off day (61). All those who climb the Window Buttress enter it, and the crest of this massive tower, which by the way reminds one of the Parson's Nose in Snowdonia, affords a commanding view of it. Others may find plenty of scrambling on the shattered face of the corrie, but unless they are rock-climbers, should avoid the gully immediately below the bealach. If they wish to reach this great cleft in the ridge they will make the first steep ascent and then climb the scree gully on the right below the cliffs of Sgurr Dearg, traversing to the left thereafter until the bealach is attained.

Coire na Creiche may be visited by all those walking between Glen Brittle and Sligachan in either direction (62). Apart from its wild grandeur as a whole, its most important feature of interest to the rock-climber is the Waterpipe Gully which splits the face of Sgurr an Fheadain. It is 1,300 feet (396 m) high, contains over twenty pitches, and was first climbed in 1895 by Kelsall and Hallitt. The best time to ascend it is in dry weather when the 'pipe' is empty; whereas after a deluge waterfalls empty themselves into it throughout its entire height with the burn at its exit a couple of feet (·6 m) deep. This gully is one of the three longest in Britain. The others are also in Scotland: the Chasm on Buachaille Etive Mor and the Clachaig Gully at the western end of Glencoe, immediately above the inn.

Sgurr an Fheadain stands at the end of a short lateral ridge which merges with the Main Ridge at Bidein Druim nan Ramh, thus dividing the upper part of Coire na Creiche into two smaller corries. The curious point about them is that Coir'a'Mhadaidh is on the left, and Tairneilear on the right, when the names should surely be interchanged so that the former is immediately below its own great peaks.

Plate 57 Sron na Ciche

Plate 58 Sgurr Alasdair and Sgumain from Coire Lagan

Plate 59 Massive boiler plates of Coire a' Ghrunnda

Plate 60 Sgurr Alasdair from Coire a' Ghrunnda

Plate 61 Coire na Banachdich

Rubh'an Dunain is the long promontory jutting out into the sea
some 4 miles (7 km) south of Glen Brittle, and strangely enough
the walk to it by the shore of Loch Brittle is usually regarded as a
mere off-day jaunt. Just what is meant by an 'off' day I have
never discovered: if it implies a lazy day after many energetic
days on the hills, then I am in agreement; but if it means a day
when the weather is too bad for mountaineering, then I would
say keep indoors and don't go down to Rubh'an Dunain, but
reserve for it a bright sunny afternoon when you can laze about
on its cliffs and enjoy the glorious tang of the breeze.

I invited Mr. and Mrs. Fenwick to accompany me on this walk
and we left the Lodge together on a morning that promised well.
A clearly-marked track skirts the south-east shore of Loch Brittle
and is gained from any point near the cottages which nestle by
the bay. After the recent rains we found this path decidedly wet
and boggy until it climbed higher up the cliffs which are
prominent in the view down the loch. Skirting these craggy
heights we came to the wall extending right across the neck of the
promontory, and crossed it at a convenient break. Thereafter the
moorland falls gently towards Rubh'an Dunain and is intersected
by streams going in all directions. We made for one of the stooks
of rock where we arranged ourselves comfortably and ate our
sandwiches. We did not linger since we were anxious to explore
as much as possible of the sea edge during the afternoon, and so
took a direct line for the point, passing Loch na h'Airde on the
way.

The coastline hereabouts is fascinating. Black weathered rocks
rise sheer from the sea and form rough plateaux, sometimes with
occasional patches of sparse grass thereon, but more often
completely bare. Everywhere they contain rounded holes full of
sea water and are cracked and broken by the ceaseless pounding
of the tides, whilst behind them rise basaltic columns whose tops
merge with the heathery moorland (65).

We sat on the edge of the cliffs and scanned the great expanse
of ocean in search of a white sail or the smoke trail of a steamer,

but in their absence our eyes were led again and again to the dim
blue outlines of Rhum and Canna, or to the hills of Soay just
across the Sound. The warm sunshine, the gentle breeze and the
ceaseless murmur of the sea almost lulled us off to dreamland,
until the sudden flight of a cormorant would bring us back to
reality. We rose to continue our stroll along the edge of these
cliffs, and passing many a tiny cove littered with debris, wended
our way to the Dun. My companions went ahead whilst I
scrambled over the slippery seaweed between the maze of
boulders, to toy with my camera at each changing viewpoint, and
after climbing a nearby crag, to snap them at the end of the
promontory (64). I then went round to join them, and from the
cairn standing on the Dun was able to look along the shattered
cliffs fringing the Sound, and to see the low hills of Strathaird
about Elgol rising across the waters of Loch Scavaig (66).

Turning our steps homewards, we skirted the shore of Loch na
h'Airde whose distant background was formed by the great cliffs
frowning upon Loch Brittle 500 feet (152 m) below (67). It was
pleasant wandering back over the boggy moorland, here and
there relieved by a tiny lochan, blue in the sunshine and girt with
rock. We had hoped to view the corries from these tumbled
uplands but they were still obscured by a great white cloud which
huddled round the Coolins like a gigantic ball of cotton wool and
seemed immovable in the fresh breeze. Descending from the last
craggy hill to the path by the shore of Loch Brittle (68), we
walked back to the Lodge with the music of many a tiny
waterfall in our ears (69), well satisfied with this easy day in the
very shadow of the hills.

Plate 63 Rhum and Rubh' an Dunain from Sgurr nan Gobhar

Plate 64 Rubh'an Dunain

Plate 65 The western seaboard

Plate 66 Soay Sound from the Dun

Plate 68 Loch Brittle

Loch Coruisk is perhaps the greatest tourist attraction in the Coolins. It has received much notice from writers, poets, painters and photographers, and since it lies so near the head of Loch Scavaig, is easily visited by boat from Glen Brittle and Elgol and also from any passing steamer. I made three unsuccessful attempts to catch it in a mood to justify its fame, two of them by the long walk from Sligachan when it either rained or sleeted, and one by boat from Glen Brittle when the cloud, haze and gloom revealed it as most wayfarers see it.

On the present occasion no regular boat service was in operation from Glen Brittle, but six of us were able to arrange for the hire of a craft from the lobster fishermen of Soay. We had asked for it at ten a.m. but owing to motor trouble it did not arrive until two hours later. There was a stiff wind blowing from the south-west, and as the motor was not functioning properly, it took us two hours to get to Loch Scavaig. The approach to its head is magnificent with the steep flanks of Gars-bheinn towering up on the left and those of Sgurr na Stri rising to a lesser height on the right. Its edge consists of vast boiler plates covered with seaweed which afford an insecure foothold and whose sides dip down below water at a precipitous angle revealing the sea bed twenty or thirty feet (6 m to 9 m) below.

The landing point is near the river which flows over these boiler plates to empty Loch Coruisk, and a rough path follows its twisting course to the loch's outflow. Here the scene is grand and impressive with the loch hemmed in on all sides by bare rock whose cliffs fall steeply to its shore. Those on the left consist of the vast expanse of boiler plates flanking the great ridge of the Dubhs (71), and those on the right support the long high ridge of Druim nan Ramh, whilst across the distant background stretch the massive peaks of the Coolins whose skyline reveals to advantage Sgurrs a'Ghreadaidh, Mhadaidh and Bidein Druim nan Ramh. A better viewpoint, however, is from the top of the vast heap of piled up boiler plates flanking Sgurr na Stri. Here the full two miles (3·38 km) of Coruisk are disclosed at one's feet together with the deep recesses of Coir-uisg which lie at its head (70). The best viewpoint of all is the summit of Sgurr na Stri itself which I have referred to elsewhere.

Plate 70 Loch Coruisk

Plate 71 Meall na Cuilce and the Dubhs

Even in Skye climbers sometimes take more than one 'off' day from the Coolins and go further afield to see some of the other spectacular features of the island, such as the Storr or Quiraing. But the coast itself in the far west merits a visit *in any weather* as it is resplendent with cliffs that drop sheer into the seething Atlantic. Here Waterstein Head dominates the wild scene with its 971 feet (296 m) of precipitous rock, and is probably the magnet that draws the connoisseur, together with Neist Lighthouse opposite, which is the most westerly in Skye and is perched on the very edge of the cliffs. On the way there it is worth visiting Loch Pooltiel with its deserted pier and harbour facing the beetling cliffs of Dunvegan Head.

Coming from either Glen Brittle or Sligachan, you follow the main road to Dunvegan, with its changing picturesque seascapes on the left, and at Lonmore turn left and keep to the narrow winding road through Cobost. Near a school you cross the hills to Glendale. Thereafter you must drive carefully along the narrow road, ignoring the left branch to Ramasaig, and later keep to the right for the downhill run to Pooltiel which terminates at Meanish. Returning to the last fork, you now turn right and after passing the lonely cottages at Waterstein you drive on to the car park at the end of the road, which is poised high above the sea.

Now you begin a pleasant walk by first descending the steep steps beyond the car park. Keep to the well-made path that leads to the Lighthouse. If you want a frontal view of Waterstein Head you may now stroll down grassy slopes to a rocky point opposite, and if you are a photographer the light is most favourable after 3 p.m. Moreover, while a close view of the Lighthouse may be obtained from the rocks below, its striking situation is best revealed from the sketchy track that goes uphill from the car park and ends on the edge of the cliffs, high above the ocean.

Plate 72 Loch Broglice

Plate 73 Waterstein Head, 971 ft, from the car park

Sgurr Alasdair (3,257 ft. (993 m)) dominates the whole of the
Coolins and was first climbed by the late Sheriff Alexander
Nicolson in 1873. Since this graceful peak is easily ascended by
the tourist it merits early notice. I first climbed it on a Whit
Monday when a strange stillness pervaded the atmosphere and
thin haze with a few listless clouds stretched far across the sky. I
walked up to Coire Lagan alone and when I climbed the Great
Stone Shoot, every stone that moved beneath my feet made a
sound which reverberated through this gloomy chasm to echo in
the corrie below. By taking a course, first close below the crags
on the right, and later when I entered the grim portals of the
Shoot close to those on the left, I was able to make the ascent an
easy one so that when I reached its crest I did not have to rest
before attacking the narrow *arête* of basalt which rises to the
cairn perched on the top of the peak. On emerging from the
gloomy recesses of the Shoot, the change of scene was dramatic,
revealing a striking prospect of the two higher summits of the
Dubhs together with the more distant top of Gars-bheinn where
a pennant of cloud rose skywards to sail slowly overhead in the
direction of Sgurr Dearg (75). Turning to the right, I tackled the
narrow ridge which ends on the summit of Alasdair and in the
course of its traverse discloses the abysmal depths of the Stone
Shoot immediately below. The cairn stands on the smallest top in
the Coolins and there is barely room for anyone to sit beside it
(77). A narrow arm stretches westwards for a few feet and then
the side of the mountain drops away at a sensational angle in one
seemingly unbroken precipice right down to the floor of Coire
Lagan. To the south-west a spectacular ridge falls to the *col* (78),
and rises again to Sgumain with Loch Brittle and the illimitable
sea in the background (79). To the north, and immediately
overlooking the Stone Shoot, stands Sgurr Thearlaich whose
cairn is only 50 feet (15 m) below and tops the narrow roof-like
ridge which falls steeply to the *col* below Sgurr Mhic Coinnich.
Beyond this castellated summit the flanks of Sgurr Dearg drop
precipitously into Coire Lagan and to the right of it the ridge

Plate 75 Dubhs and Gars-bheinn from the crest of the Stone Shoot

tails away to the north to end with the shapely peak of Sgurr nan Gillean.

I sat down on firm rock with my legs dangling over the Great Stone Shoot, and while poised in space, soliloquised amid the solemn grandeur and wild beauty of this impressive landscape. The silence was so profound that I could almost *feel* it, and the air was so still that the smoke from my cigarette rose in an unbroken spiral to merge with the cloud drifting slowly overhead. The atmosphere was so opalescent that it imparted a strange pearly quality to some of the unclouded peaks, but I was able to pick out every one of them from end to end of the Main Ridge. To the south-east cloud still formed on Gars-bheinn and its pennant trailed slowly over Sgurr nan Eag, then far above Coir'a' Ghrunnda, to pass overhead as a broad misty band whose penumbra imparted a black and forbidding aspect to the great precipices of Sgurr Dearg on the other side of Coire Lagan. The rest of the ridge basked in intermittent sunshine, but all the time the lovely lines of Blaven rose into the sky to the east, shimmering away in the weak sunlight to provide a scene of mountain splendour not easily forgotten by those privileged to see it (77).

The rare charm of this incomparable panorama held my gaze for two hours with no other human being in sight, although I knew some of the Good Companions were at that moment struggling with the difficulties of the Cioch Gully in the dim recesses of Sron na Ciche below. Then the great metamorphosis occurred, for while I looked down on Coire Lagan, thin wisps of mist began to curl in and out of its surrounding buttresses and gullies, to rise slowly, and finally to shroud one after the other of the adjacent peaks. Here was a scene so often observed in the Coolins, but so seldom encountered in the hills of Britain's mainland. And yet, how much more wonderful it was to perceive this transformation from above than from below, and moreover still to be clear of the now boiling mists which encompassed me. A break suddenly occurred to the north and through this glistening window I gazed out upon the northern section of the ridge where Sgurr nan Gillean rose clearly into the sky (80). I climbed down hurriedly to the crest of the Stone Shoot and there beheld another aspect of this fascinating scene (76). Then, amid the clatter of the rolling stones, I descended through stygian gloom to emerge in the sunlight once again on the floor of Coire Lagan.

Plate 76 Mist in the great Stone Shoot

Plate 78 Climbers on the *Mauvais Pas*

PLATE 70 I.—A Brittle and Strong ... from the ... North-West side.

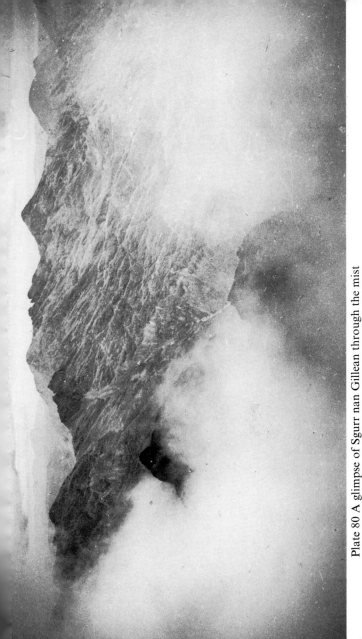

Plate 80 A glimpse of Sgurr nan Gillean through the mist

Plate 81 The Good Companions on the Cioch

The mere mention of Sron na Ciche will conjure up in the memory of the rock-climber joyous days, when he was either perched perilously upon one of its buttresses, or struggling with the problems encountered in the dim recesses of one of its deep gullies. The crag is immense: its bare face of rock towers into the sky for about 1,000 feet (305 m) at its centre and its precipices extend for about a mile on the Coire Lagan side, although they are less than this on the Coir'a'Ghrunnda face. The former is perhaps the more popular with climbers as is evidenced by the well-worn track which leads to it from Glen Brittle. It faces north-north-west so that it lies in shadow until the afternoon, when the climber may bask in the sunshine and so be tempted to linger there until well into the evening and to get back to Glen Brittle too late to enjoy the sumptuous repast awaiting him.

The top of this great escarpment slopes to the south-west as a stony plateau, littered with boulders, and having its cairn 2,817 feet (859 m) above sea level. The whole of it consists of rough gabbro, intersected by basaltic dykes, which, owing to their more rapid erosion, have formed the gullies and the chimneys festooning the face of the crag. A conspicuous terrace runs steeply across its face with an upward slope from east to west and from a distance appears to be continuous. Leaving the Sgumain Stone Shoot where it begins to fan out, it crosses to the Eastern Gully above the bottom pitch and encircles the Cioch Slab as far as the Cioch Gully where a large jammed boulder forms an arch (84). An untraversed gap then appears, after which it rises to the top of the precipices near the summit of the West Buttress, passing the Flake—where there is a second hiatus—and the Finger, before emerging on the skyline. These cliffs were first explored by the late Professor Collie as long ago as 1906 and have since become the favourite playground of the rock-climber in the whole of the Coolins.

The most remarkable feature of Sron na Ciche is the Cioch, a gigantic boss of gabbro projecting from the Cioch Slab and having its sloping roof at a height of 2,300 feet (701 m). It is

Plate 82 Climbing the Cioch

Plate 83 Descending the Cioch

Plate 84 Cioch Gully—the Arch

most easily ascended from the Terrace by climbing the deep, well nail-marked crack, rising from the left corner of the Slab and ending in the Eastern Gully just above the second pitch. A short scramble then leads to a conspicuous shelf on the right, which lower down opens out on to an easy ledge and thence falls to the narrow neck behind the Cioch (82). The easiest way from the neck to its roof is by two short chimneys followed by a traverse. Those who wish to avoid the Eastern Gully may do so by climbing a stiff crack which leads direct to the shelf.

On the present occasion, Fenwick and I descended from Coire Lagan, and after circling the base of Sgumain, entered the Eastern Gully by the lower section of the Terrace which is here so shattered that we traversed the wall above it. Ascending the scree to the second pitch which has so far not been climbed, we roped up and Fenwick led by way of the crack, ledge and hand traverse on its left wall which brought us to the top of the jammed boulder. We then unroped and followed the route above described. On descending the ledge to the Cioch we hailed three of the Good Companions who were just emerging from the Cioch Gully and while I remained behind to take a number of photographs, they all climbed on to the sloping roof of this strange pinnacle (81). During their descent I snapped them again (83), and we were then lowered down the top pitch of the Cioch Gully, the last man abseiling down to join us in the Cave. We escaped from this damp recess by scrambling down to the Arch and then walked round the Terrace to rejoin the track descending to Glen Brittle (84).

from Gars-Bheinn to Sgurr Dearg

Those who set out to traverse the southern section of the Main
Ridge will have to allow a good three hours in which to reach
Gars-bheinn from Glen Brittle. The walk over the moorland with
its lochans, burns, bogs and boulders, encircles the flanks of the
whole of the southern group, and its many ups and downs seem
endless until the Allt Coire nan Laogh is crossed and the steep
scree tackled. Once the cairn on Gars-bheinn is attained the real
charm of the expedition begins, for you stand here on this great
sentinel looking down on the waters of Loch Scavaig far below,
with Soay also at your feet and Eigg, Rhum and Canna away
across the channel.

The walk throughout is exhilarating, with first the rough
undulations of Sgurr a'Choire Bhig, after which you drop down
to the *col* and then scramble up the shattered slopes of Sgurr nan
Eag. Looking back from here you obtain a comprehensive idea
of the ridge you have just traversed (86), and when you attain the
flat broad crest of this mountain, the next section of the traverse
is disclosed before you with the isolated Caisteal a'Gharbh-choire
below, Sgurr Dubh an Da Bheinn rising on its right, and its
continuation to Sgurr Thearlaich on the right of Sgurr Alasdair
(87).

As you walk gaily along this high roof you will notice the
lochan cradled in Coir' a'Ghrunnda below on the left. The crest
of the Stone Shoot appears on the right and separates it from the
top of Sgurr Thearlaich, beyond which are the summits of the
distant Sgurrs a'Ghreadaidh and Mhadaidh (85).

The long crest of Sgurr nan Eag is almost level and when you
come to the end of it, the first difficult bit of scrambling is
encountered. If, however, you wish to avoid this you may do so
by descending slightly on the Ghrunnda side to thread your way
in and out of the maze of large boulders. Gaining the ridge again
at the bottom of this section, you walk along an easy stretch with
Caisteal a'Gharbh-choire ahead (88). This strange obstacle,
consisting of Peridotite, is the roughest bit of gabbro in the
Coolins. It provides a short, stiff climb of about 60 feet (18 m);

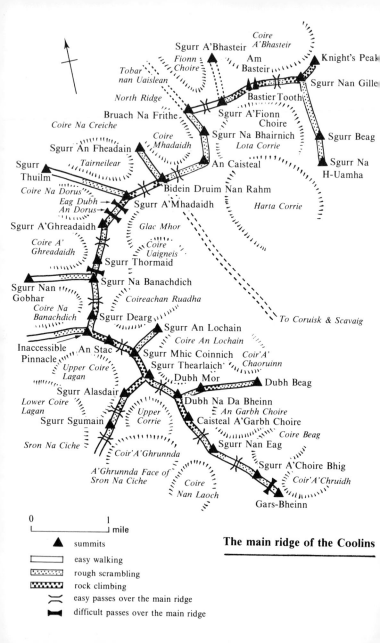

The main ridge of the Coolins

Coire
A'Bhasteir

Sgurr A'Bhasteir

Fionn
Choire

Am
Basteir

Knight's Peak

Tobar
nan Uaislean

Sgurr Nan Gille

North Ridge

Bastier Tooth

Bruach Na Frithe

Sgurr A'Fionn
Choire

Coire Na Creiche

Sgurr Na Bhairnich

Sgurr Beag

Coire
Mhadaidh

Lota Corrie

Sgurr An Fheadain

Sgurr Na
H-Uamha

Tairneilear

An Caisteal

Sgurr
Thuilm

Coire Na Dorus

Bidein Druim Nan Rahm

Eag Dubh
An Dorus

Sgurr A'Mhadaidh

Harta Corrie

Sgurr A'Ghreadaidh

Glac Mhor

Coire A'
Ghreadaidh

Coire
Uaigneis

Sgurr Thormaid

Sgurr Na Banachdich

Sgurr Nan
Gobhar

Coireachan Ruadha

Coire Na
Banachdich

Sgurr Dearg

To Coruisk & Scavaig

Sgurr An Lochain

Coire An Lochain

Inaccessible
Pinnacle

An Stac

Sgurr Mhic Coinnich

Coir'A'
Chaoruinn

Upper Coire
Lagan

Sgurr Thearlaich

Dubh Mor

Dubh Beag

Sgurr Alasdair

Dubh Na Da Bheinn

Lower Coire
Lagan

An Garbh Choire

Sgurr Sgumain

Upper
Corrie

Caisteal A'Garbh Choire

Sron Na Ciche

Coire Beag

Sgurr Nan Eag

Coir'A'Ghrunnda

Sgurr A'Choire Bhig

A'Ghrunnda Face of
Sron Na Ciche

Coire
Nan Laoch

Coir'A'Chruidh

Gars-Bheinn

0   1
|___|___|___|___|___|___| mile

▲ summits

▭ easy walking

▨ rough scrambling

▧ rock climbing

⟩⟨ easy passes over the main ridge

▶◀ difficult passes over the main ridge

but if you wish to turn it, you may do so by traversing the scree
on either side. This leads to a rough terrace crossing the slopes of
Sgurr Dubh an Da Bheinn but it is usual to take in this peak in
the traverse, and after descending its far side you cross the
Bealach Coire an Lochain where the difficult climbing begins.
Unless you are an expert or with a party of experienced rock-
climbers you will be well advised to leave the Main Ridge and
traverse the scree *below* Alasdair to the *col* between it and
Sgumain, where an easy way leads home. If, however, you keep
to the ridge you scramble up the steep crags of the Pinnacle
overhanging the short side of the Thearlaich-Dubh Gap and 30
feet (9 m) high (89). You can perhaps abseil down the precipice
of this formidable cleft but the climb on the long side of it is 80
feet (24 m) high and, when you have reached the top, an easy
scramble follows to the cairn on Sgurr Thearlaich. You may of
course do the usual thing by taking in Alasdair before scaling it,
when the airy walk down its crest will take you to the Mhic
Coinnich *col*. Here the top of this mountain soars skywards and
you may climb the sporting course up King's Chimney or avoid
it by traversing the obvious Collies Ledge which starts about 20
feet (6 m) above the *col*, and slanting up to the left, passes
round the knob to bring you to the ridge again just north of the
summit (90). The long back of this sharp ridge leads down to the
Bealach Coire Lagan and you are now faced with the steep
buttress of An Stac projecting from Sgurr Dearg underneath the
Inaccessible Pinnacle. If you wish to avoid these two difficult
obstacles also, you may keep to the scree on the Coire Lagan side
and thus attain the cairn of Sgurr Dearg (91).

Plate 85 Sgurr Alasdair and Coire a'Ghrunnda from Sgurr nan Eag

Plate 86 Sgurr a'Choire Bhig and Gars-bheinn

Plate 88 Caisteal a'Gharbh-Choire, Gars-bheinn and Sgurr nan Eag from Sgumain

Plate 89 The Theorlaich Dubh Gap, Blaven and the Dubbs

Plate 90 Sgurr Mhic Coinnich with the main ridge beyond

Plate 91 Sgurr Dearg and Sgurr a'Ghreadaidh from Sgumain

This section of the Main Ridge rises immediately to the east of Glen Brittle and its terminal points are thus within easy reach. On a calm day its traverse affords no difficulties but under wild conditions the three narrow tops of Sgurr na Banachdich may be turned by keeping immediately below their crests on the west side of the mountain. The circuit of Coire na Banachdich includes this part of the main Ridge and while there is not much to choose between the directions in which it is taken, I think the advantages to the photographer lie with the ascent of Sgurr nan Gobhar and the descent of the long shoulder of Sgurr Dearg, because he is then on the latter peak in the afternoon when the lighting of the most important scenes, including that of the magnificent Alasdair group, is most favourable. Since, however, a description of the ridge in the reverse direction is necessary for the sake of continuity in this work, I shall write of it this way, although it will be understood that the camera studies which accompany this section were secured by going from north to south.

Leave Glen Brittle by the Coire Lagan track, and after passing Eas Mor, advance straight towards the shoulder of the mountain (92). Here masses of scree make the ascent rather trying, but on reaching a conspicuous dyke below the first point on the ridge the going becomes easier. Beyond this small top the angle is reduced and you cross a vast expanse of scree whilst making direct for Sron Dearg, looking rather like a giant castle poised high on the ridge and extending right across it. The views down into Coire na Banachdich are impressive, whilst those of Sron na Ciche on the right reveal its whole face clearly, especially the Terrace which rises diagonally from left to right. There is no easy way to the top of Sron Dearg, although you may be tempted to go over to the right. When you reach its cairn the narrow shattered continuation of the ridge is seen ahead. On tackling this, you will pass some sensational drops and one or two places which are rather slippery, but this section is soon traversed and you then walk forward to the summit ridge of Sgurr Dearg.

The most magnificent prospect is on your right where you look across Coire Lagan to its engirdling ridge dominated by the graceful peak of Sgurr Alasdair. This superb skyline from left to right includes Sgurr Mhic Coinnich and Sgurr Thearlaich with the Dubhs appearing in the gap between them. The whole of the Great Stone Shoot is visible and, to the right of Alasdair, Sgumain seems to be leaning over towards Sron na Ciche further to the south (95). Looking now to the left of this group you will be impressed by the bold outline of An Stac, but your gaze will rest upon the Inaccessible Pinnacle whose amazing crest towers above the ridge of Sgurr Dearg (93). From the north it appears equally strange (94) but scarcely as impressive as its end elevation (96).

Continuing your walk, now on the Main Ridge, you will soon come to the northern tip of Sgurr Dearg which reveals the most striking prospect of Sgurr na Banachdich, right from the bealach below to its summit, with Thormaid and the Three Teeth and a glimpse of Sgurr Thuilm behind them (97). The panorama is superb and includes the whole of the northern Coolins (98).

The descent over scree to the Bealach Coire na Banachdich is easy and when you reach this gigantic cleft in the ridge you will see a wonderful vista of Blaven framed by its precipitous walls (99). The ascent of Banachdich now commences, first at an easy angle where the ridge is broad, and thereafter much steeper where it narrows. The views down to Coir-uisg on the right are sensational and, if a gale of wind is blowing from the west, you will be well advised to keep away from its edge.

On reaching the summit you bear to the left and follow the cairns down the scree slope which leads to the rocky crest of Sgurr nan Gobhar. The going here will remind you of Striding Edge on Helvellyn. The descent to Glen Brittle is at first rough, but the moorland is soon encountered and a direct line taken for the Lodge.

Plate 92 Sgurr Dearg from Eas Mor

Plate 94 Sgurr Alasdair and the Inaccessible Pinnacle from the North

Plate 95 Sgurr Alasdair from Sgurr Dearg

Plate 96 The Inaccessible Pinnacle

Plate 97 The Banachdich Ridge from Dearg

Plate 98 Sgurr a'Ghreadaidh and the ridge to Sgurr nan Gillean

Plate 99 Blaven from Bealach Coire na Banachdich

Plate 100 Ghreadaidh and Thormaid from Banachdich

This section of the Main Ridge is usually regarded as one of the climbers' tit-bits; not so much because it is particularly difficult or dangerous (although anyone who fell off it would not return to tell the tale), but more especially because parts of its crest are the narrowest and most spectacular in the whole of the Coolins. It extends from Sgurr na Banachdich in the south to Sgurr a'Mhadaidh in the north, and includes Sgurr Thormaid as well as Sgurr a'Ghreadaidh which occupies a superb position with views looking right down the full length of Loch Coruisk. Any of the usual routes may be followed to the summit of Sgurr na Banachdich, but its best finish is over the long high lateral ridge of Sgurr Thuilm, which, however, is followed by a trying descent over extensive scree slopes, but afterwards by a pleasant walk over the moor back to Glen Brittle.

All the Good Companions wished to do this traverse, but as I was especially anxious to choose a good day when I should not have to wait for the light, two of them embarked upon it before my party, and on their return gave us a vivid account of their experiences. One of them, who shall be nameless, was a born *raconteur*, for he had that command of language and lilt of voice, that glance of eye and turn of the head, which holds the attention of his listeners. In the course of his adventurous story of the traverse, which was made from north to south, he told us how on reaching the summit ridge of Sgurr a'Ghreadaidh he and his companion had roped up and in one place crossed a very slippery slab, in another swung themselves across a gap to a projecting knob of rock, and in yet another had looked down to see Coruisk framed between their legs! After this sensational account we had some trepidation in following in their footsteps, but when we came to traverse this particular section of the ridge on the following day, we neither used a rope nor found these *mauvais pas* difficult, and were therefore forced to the conclusion that our legs had been well and truly pulled!

The next morning dawned with a cloudless sky and without a breath of wind in the glen, so immediately after breakfast I set off with Atkinson and Fenwick to climb Sgurr na Banachdich. We took the easier route which goes round the base of Sgurr nan Gobhar, and after scaling the steep scree of Coir'an Eich, reached the summit of this mountain in two hours. The vista in all directions was entrancing with the nearer islands and the Outer Hebrides floating on a placid gleaming sea. A certain amount of haze already dimmed the prospect, as also that of the jagged peaks of the Coolins which stretched away in the distance on either hand. While my companions rested by the cairn I toyed with my camera, but instead of hanging on to the edge of the narrow ridge with my hands as I had done on a previous occasion when a sleety gale from the west had swept over it, I was able to walk about with considerable ease. From the northern tip of Sgurr na Banachdich I looked down upon the route we were to follow and perceived the pointed top of Sgurr Thormaid just below, with the sharp serrated edge of the Three Teeth beyond it, the ridge finally sweeping up in one long curve to the almost horizontal summit of Sgurr a'Ghreadaidh (100).

We commenced the traverse by scrambling down the shattered terminus of Sgurr na Banachdich, and on reaching the little *col* below gazed up at the steep crest of Thormaid which we climbed on its left with sensational drops beneath us. Looking back from the cairn, the vast precipices of Banachdich swept down in a long series of gigantic broken slabs to the floor of Coireachan Ruadha below (101). The northern face of Thormaid is slabby and not so steep as its opposite side so we were able to walk down to the Teeth which were traversed by Fenwick whilst Atkinson and I crossed the ledge below them on the west (102). The scene ahead of us was magnificent for the ridge of Ghreadaidh soared skywards like the curving blade of a titanic scimitar. We tackled it with gusto and were able to make rapid progress because the innumerable small ledges of gabbro provided good holds for both hands and feet and imbued us with a sense of security such as is not experienced upon any other type of rock in the country. Up and up we went, keeping to the crest of the ridge all the way, with the steep shattered face of the mountain on our left and its smooth precipitous slabs dropping out of sight on our right. In a

Plate 101 Banachdich from Thormaid

Plate 102 We walk down to the Three Teeth

surprisingly short time we had reached the south top and were standing by its cairn scanning the knife-edge ridge ahead.

Here was a scene that would appeal to any mountaineer: a seemingly impossible ridge poised in the sky and festooned between the twin summits of a giant peak; on one side its shattered cliffs dropping away at a terrifically steep angle and on the other immense slabs of rock sloping downwards precipitously to abysmal depths. Nor was this all, for there was the vastness of space, the sense of isolation, the thrill of height, the magic of solemn beauty, the impressiveness of a brooding silence, and a solitude that filled the soul.

We began to move across the ridge one at a time, my companions noiselessly in their rubber shoes while my boots made familiar sounds as the nails rasped sharply against the rough gabbro. Sometimes we walked on its crest when it was wide enough, while at others we traversed the narrow ledges immediately beneath it on one side or the other. There were a few awkward bits where great care was vital and we were amused at one place, where the edge was undercut, by imagining a fat man performing all sorts of gyrations to pass it in safety (103). On reaching the centre we paused to admire the setting of Coruisk, framed like a flashing jewel between the V-shaped walls of the opening. Continuing our traverse we attained the higher cairn all too soon and there sat in the sunshine, revelling in the beauty of the splendid prospect of the northern end of the Main ridge (104).

On the north side of this summit a massive wart of rock rises from the ridge, and since it appeared to be a comfortable spot near which to eat our lunch, we walked down to it and for half an hour quietly enjoyed the views in the warm sunshine. Continuing our traverse, the descent now lost much of its exhilaration because the crest of the ridge broadened and was at a comparatively easy angle. At the narrow gap of Eag Dubh we followed the wiser course of skirting its edge, instead of risking a leap across it, and soon reached An Dorus where a nice climb down a twenty-foot wall led us to the floor of the chasm.

The South West peak of Sgurr a'Mhadaidh rises sheer on the

other side of this *col* and keeping to the crest of the ridge all the
way, we duly arrived at the cairn. Looking back from here
disclosed a prospect of the colossal slabs of Sgurr a'Ghreadaidh
with the shadowy gap of Eag Dubh cutting their edge and
Atkinson carefully negotiating the slabs immediately below us
(105). This peak is the highest of the four tops of Mhadaidh and
is characterised by a horizontal crest of rock 30 feet (9 m) long.
From its far end a good idea is obtained of the steepness of its
face (106), which on the north side drops just as precipitously to
Tairneilear at its base. Moreover, the peak is a splendid
viewpoint for the appraisal of the vast basin cradling Coruisk, at
the other end of which Sgurr na Stri overlooks its outflow, whilst
it is flanked on the west by the great slabs rising to Sgurr Dubh
Beag (107). The other three tops of Mhadaidh are also revealed
to advantage with the track on the right of the third peak rising
to its summit. On the left of the fourth peak there is a glimpse of
Bidein Druim nan Ramh, while Blaven forms the everpresent
background (108). While Atkinson and I sat on the summit
scanning this vast landscape, Fenwick made a quick traverse of
all the Mhadaidh tops, and on rejoining us we left the Main
Ridge to traverse Sgurr Thuilm (109).

The north-west face of Sgurr a'Mhadaidh is spectacular. A
long narrow buttress of great steepness forms the ridge and is
flanked on the south by a short chimney and on the north by
Deep Gash Gully which is of sensational proportions and has
never been climbed. Fenwick descended this buttress alone while
Atkinson and I turned it on the south to rejoin him at the *col*
below. We then ascended the narrow shattered ridge leading to
the summit of Sgurr Thuilm and on looking back obtained a
splendid vista of the ground covered on our descent (110), and of
that of the Main Ridge we had traversed earlier in the day. The
view disclosed the broken structure of the slopes enclosing Coire
a'Ghreadaidh and also gave us our last glimpse of Alasdair and
Dearg (111).

We picked our way carefully down the seemingly interminable
scree slopes of Thuilm, and making for the burn below, drank to
our full of its cold, peaty water. Following the stream down we

Plate 103 Traversing the narrow summit ridge of Ghreadaidh

came in due course to a pool whose cool clear water exercised an irresistible attraction upon us. Fenwick was the first to undress, but the water was so cold that he did not immerse himself above the knees. A paddle, therefore, had to suffice and so ended for us all a perfect day on the magic hills of Skye (112).

Plate 104 Bruach na Frithe, Sgurr nan Gillean and (below) Bidein Druim nan Ramh from the North top

Plate 105 The North ridge of Ghreadaidh from Mhadaidh

Plate 106 The South-West peak of Mhadaidh and the two tops of Ghreadaidh

Plate 107 Loch Coruisk from Sgurr a'Mhadaidh

Plate 108 Bidein and the three subsidiary tops of Mhadaidh with Blaven beyond

Plate 109 Sgurr Thuilm from Sgurr a'Mhadaidh

Plate 110 Sgurr a'Mhadaidh from Sgurr Thuilm

Plate 111 Coire a'Ghreadaidh from Sgurr Thuilm

Plate 112 The end of a perfect day

Plate 113 Bruach na Frithe from Sgurr Bhairnich

On the morrow I moved to Sligachan with the object of spending a few days on the northern section of the Main Ridge, but my arrival signalled a drastic change in the weather, for the rains came and continued to pour almost incessantly for three long weeks. During much of this time the hills were curtained with low cloud and the moors became saturated so that scarcely a dry spot could be found. The playful burns poured down in a series of noisy cataracts, whilst the River Sligachan, now in spate, swept along in one wild rush almost to reach the arches of the bridge near the inn. On some days I walked up into the corries, groping my way blindly in and out of the chaotically arranged boulders but on attaining the bealachs I found the same blanket of mist and rain on the other side of them; on others I scaled the various lateral ridges, only to return to my hotel drenched to the skin. When the watery sky assumed a less leaden appearance I ventured out on the Main Ridge and on four occasions unsuccessfully attempted its traverse from Bidein Druim nan Ramh to Bruach na Frithe, and on only two of these did the sun enable me to catch glimpses of its splendour.

The section dealt with in this monograph stretches from Sgurr a'Mhadaidh to Bruach na Frithe, and whilst the ridge is not particularly narrow, it nevertheless includes some climbing on the Bidein group whose three tops form a rough triangle. Starting from the south-west peak of Mhadaidh it runs eastwards as far as the central peak of Bidein and then turns northwards taking in An Caisteal and Sgurr Bhairnich before rising to Bruach na Frithe. The topography of the central part is worthy of note because Bidein is the only peak in the Coolins supported by four well defined ridges. Two of these are, of course, the Main Ridge already mentioned, whereas on the north the short lateral ridge from Sgurr an Fheadain joins it, and on the south the long ridge of Druim nan Ramh connects it more or less continuously with the small peak of Sgurr na Stri.

Those who wish to follow this section will leave Sligachan by the path which rises from the Allt Dearg cottage to the Bealach a'Mhaim. Before reaching the cairn, however, they will desert the track, and making for Coire na Creiche, skirt the long shoulder of Bruach na Frithe passing thereafter to one side or the other of Sgurr an Fheadain to attain the Bealach na Glac Moire just on the west side of Bidein. The climbing commences almost at once and the most difficult bit is on the north side of the Central Peak. Once the summit of the North Peak is reached the route can be seen stretching away to Bruach na Frithe and most of it is nothing more than a good scramble. A broad shelf on the west side of An Caisteal (114) leads to the great gash, a conspicuous feature in this part of the ridge, with its base 200 feet (61 m) below. A steep scree slope rises to a pinnacle below Sgurr Bhairnich but it may be turned by a ledge on the left; another gully is then crossed, and the summit of the latter easily reached. This strange hump, which appears to lean over towards Lota Corrie (116), affords a grand view of the further section of the ridge with all its broken shelves of rock sloping down to the right (113). A short scramble leads down to the ridge again which thereafter provides an easy walk until the final rocks of Bruach na Frithe are encountered. Looking back from here discloses the twist in the ridge in the foreground backed by the Dubhs and Alasdair (115) whereas the eastern prospect clearly reveals the great sloping slabs of rock which support the strange top of Sgurr a'Fionn Choire with Sgurr nan Gillean on its right (117).

A short scramble now places the climber by the cairn on Bruach na Frithe, one of the finest viewpoints in the Coolins because it affords a striking prospect of the three great bends in the Main Ridge to the south. Going first to the left this section ends with Sgurr Bhairnich; it then turns to the right over An Caisteal and Bidein Druim nan Ramh to Sgurr a'Mhadaidh; where it again bends to the left over Sgurr a'Ghreadaidh, Dearg and Alasdair to Gars-bheinn, the latter section being partly hidden by the Dubhs ridge (118). This vantage point is also a good one for the view of Blaven because the whole of its precipitous western front is seen above the gap between Sgurr Beag and Sgurr na h'Uamha (119).

Plate 114 An Caisteal and Bidein Druim nan Ramh

Plate 115 The Dubhs and Alasdair beyond the twist in the ridge

Plate 116 Sgurr Bhairnich (extreme left) to Bidein (extreme right)

Plate 117 Sgurr a'Fionn Choire and Sgurr nan Gillean from the ridge below Bruach na Frithe

Plate 118 The three bends in the main ridge seen from Bruach na Frithe

Seen from Sligachan at any time of day Sgurr nan Gillean provides a magnificent picture of mountain splendour. If you wander from the hotel on a sunny morning and follow the banks of the Sligachan River for a few yards you will see it, beyond the tumbling cascades of this boulder-strewn burn, soaring into the heavens as a majestic cone of bare rock far above the intervening stretches of billowy moorland. It seldom rises into a cloudless sky, and indeed looks much more beautiful when the great cloud galleons sweep over it, casting fascinating shadows upon the moor, and throwing into sharp relief the strange outline of Am Basteir and its Tooth which protrude from the ridge between it and Sgurr a' Bhasteir (120).

At sundown, on a favourable day, you gaze upon the scene spellbound, for Sgurr nan Gillean then stands silhouetted against the blazing sky whilst the last rays of the setting sun paint its western precipices in glowing shades of rose. As you look on this moving pageant, the shadow of Sgurr a'Bhasteir climbs the steep slopes of the mountain to dim these subtle hues until it finally appears as a black forbidding sentinel poised in the starry sky.

On the present tour my first sight of Sgurr nan Gillean will linger long in my memory, for it was then lightly decked with snow and made an inspiring picture in the brilliant sunlight (138). When I returned to Sligachan, however, it had assumed a very grim aspect which recurred daily throughout much of the three weeks alluded to in the last section. One Sunday morning during this period I had a pleasant surprise for the night had transformed it as I have portrayed it here (120), and I lost no time in collecting my sandwiches and sallying forth to climb it. I chose the Tourist Route because this way is known to climbers and wayfarers alike, and, moreover, it discloses the best views of the mountain.

The path leaves the Carbost road a few yards from the hotel and, after passing the power house, crosses the burn by a bridge and then meanders over the moorland in a direct line with the peak. In due course I came to the now familiar Allt Dearg Beag.

Plate 120 Sgurr nan Gillean from the Sligachan Burn

Throughout this part of the walk across the moor the profile of Sgurr nan Gillean does not change much except to become slightly foreshortened. The Pinnacle Ridge rises on this side of it, but the deep clefts which make it so spectacular are not seen until the south-eastern ridge of the mountain is attained. The path rises along the banks of the burn by many a lovely cascade, but I did not desert it until I reached a point opposite the obvious dip in the Nead na h'Iolaire which shuts out the view to the south. Crossing the burn, I made my way over the trackless bog towards this dip and soon reached the cairn at the other end, on the edge of Coire Riabhach. Here a stony track skirts the western slopes of the corrie and reveals its tiny lochan gleaming below, with mighty Blaven dominating Glen Sligachan to the south-east (121).

On the other side of Coire Riabhach the track steepens and the harder work begins. Cairns in plenty mark its course as its twists in and out of the wilderness of boulders and scree lying at the base of the long Pinnacle Ridge. Ahead towers the shattered but almost horizontal skyline of the South-east Ridge. Instead of following the usual route of ascent, I bore to the left and took a rising diagonal line for the diminutive peak of Sgurr Beag. As I climbed, the striking topography of the Pinnacle Ridge became apparent with Sgurr nan Gillean towering above its fourth and third pinnacles which seemed to lean over towards it beneath the great masses of swiftly moving cloud (122). When I set foot on the crest of the Ridge the true scale of this peak and its satellites was clearly revealed and I could easily perceive all the salient features of the northern section of the Main Coolins Ridge stretching away to the left and enclosing the vast basin of Lota Corrie. Far to the west the summit of Bruach na Frithe peeped over the contorted rocks of Sgurr a'Fionn Choire; then came the tip of the Bhasteir Tooth, just visible behind Am Basteir. The Bealach was the lowest point in the serrated skyline whose jagged edge passed over the 'Policeman', poised insecurely at the base of the Western Ridge, and then rose steeply to end at the pointed top of Sgurr nan Gillean whose two pinnacles on the right completed the picture (123).

Plate 121 Cloud piling up on Blaven seen from Coire Riabhach

Plate 122 Sgurr nan Gillean from the South-East

I turned my steps northwards to follow the crest of the South-east Ridge and, after passing the cairn marking the Tourist Route, commenced the final ascent. At first the going was rough but easy and when I encountered the steeper section I kept to its crest, which afforded plenty of exhilarating scrambling with precipitous drops on either side. The last hundred feet (30 m) was quite exciting but the trusty gabbro inspired confidence and I soon surmounted the narrow neck which placed me on the small summit platform (124). Although the cairn here stands on a larger top than Sgurr Alasdair, I think it conveys the sense of isolation better than any other mountain top in the country, since no part of its supporting ridges can be seen and one feels poised in the sky and aloof from the turmoil of life far below.

When I left the broader ridge near Sgurr Beag I had noticed a storm approaching from the south. The hills on the mainland were black with cloud and flashes of lightning illuminated the distant arms of the sea. As soon as I reached the cairn I turned round to scan the scene anew, only to find the heavy clouds already canopying the great mass of Blaven with obvious signs of approaching rain, whilst the streams in Glen Sligachan gleamed faintly in the half-light (125). Turning to the left I looked down upon the Pinnacle Ridge where two parties were climbing, one of them on Knight's Peak, and the other on the adjacent third pinnacle. I then crossed over to peer down the Western Ridge where the last gleam of sunlight that day cast its rays upon the overhanging mass of Am Basteir, backed by Sgurr a'Fionn Choire and Bruach na Frithe (126).

I left the top regretfully, and picking my way carefully in the rain which was now falling, commenced the descent of the tricky Western Ridge. This is a climb of moderate difficulty and is well nail-marked by the hundreds of mountaineers who have descended it. Parts of it are fairly exposed and provide the thrill of height which is so exhilarating, but the difficult part is to get off the ridge at the bottom and I chose Nicolson's Chimney as the easier course. Since I was alone and carrying a rucksack, this proved a little awkward because the wet rock was so slippery, but I reached the scree below in safety and crept into a small cave to

shelter from the rain. When the storm abated, I contoured round
to the Bealach a'Bhasteir and looked through a gap in the clouds
to see Harta Corrie far below, shut in by the long ridge of Druim
nan Ramh in the middle distance, with Gars-bheinn and the sea
beyond (128). I waited here for some time but the mist soon
began to pour over the bealach, and with the rain falling gently
once again, I turned my steps for home taking in Sgurr
a'Bhasteir on the way.

I was disappointed at the unsuccessful termination of this
traverse, and day after day went by without another opportunity
for the completion of its photography. One dull morning,
however, I had wandered up the western ridge of Sgurr
a'Bhasteir and was ambling along its summit crest when I
encountered Mr. and Mrs. J. H. Russell whom I had met
previously at Wasdale in English Lakeland. It was their first day
on the Coolins and, after penetrating the dark recesses of the Am
Basteir Corrie, they had ascended the steep scree to the Main
Ridge. While we chatted a break in the clouds appeared and Mrs.
Russell climbed the small pinnacle, just below the Bealach nan
Lice, which afforded a fine picture of wild mountain grandeur
with Sgurr na h'Uamha and the more distant Sgurr na Stri
framed in this narrow cleft in the ridge (127).

Am Basteir, familiarly known as the 'Executioner', together
with its adjacent Bhasteir Tooth, rises from the Main Ridge just
to the east of this bealach. Both of them have attained
considerable fame in the mountaineering world, not so much
because of their striking elevation, but more especially for the
difficult routes they offer the rock climber. The former is easily
ascended from the Bealach a'Bhasteir by its narrow summit ridge,
but the latter is not so accessible, although it was first climbed as
long ago as 1889 by Professor Collie, who followed a route
on the Lota Corrie side, still the easiest way to the top (129).
While examining the weird rock architecture of these main ridge
obstacles we were joined by Mr. Jim Wall, an enterprising and
fearless novice, who had made some astonishing solo ascents in
the Coolins during the previous week of bad weather. Since it
was now high time for lunch we all walked over to the cairn on

Plate 123 The main ridge from Bruach na Frithe to Sgurr nan Gillean

Sgurr a'Bhasteir where we sat and admired the spectacular structure of the Pinnacle Ridge of Sgurr nan Gillean, so well seen from this airy vantage point (130).

We spent the afternoon on the Main Ridge to the south of Bruach na Frithe, and after bidding adieu to my companions, who descended by way of Fionn Choire, I returned to Sgurr a'Bhasteir to view the scene again. The light had been very fickle throughout the afternoon and I had to wait patiently for another hour before capturing the Pinnacle Ridge in another of its changing moods (131). It was late in the evening when I left; the light had faded from Am Basteir (132), but the view to the north disclosed much of the coastline of the island from Loch Sligachan to Portree Bay, the Storr and the hills of Trotternish fading away in the distance (133). As sundown approached I came down from Sgurr a'Bhasteir and after leaving the rocks behind followed one of the streams intersecting the moor. I glanced back occasionally at the northern outposts of the Coolins now clearly outlined against the sky in the last rays of the setting sun (134).

Plate 124 Macleod's Tables and Sgurr a'Bhasteir from the summit cairn

Plate 125 The storm approaches Sgurr nan Gillean

Plate 126 Looking down the Western ridge

Plate 127 Looking South-East from Bealach nan Lice

Plate 128 A break in the clouds seen from Bealach a'Bhasteir

Plate 129 Am Basteir and the Bhasteir Tooth

Plate 130 The Pinnacle Ridge of Sgurr nan Gillean from Sgurr a'Bhasteir

Plate 131 Evening light on the Pinnacle ridge

Plate 132 Waning light on the Bhasteir ridge

Plate 133 The Trotternish Hills and the sea from Sgurr a'Bhasteir

Plate 134 The Pinnacle Ridge of Sgurr nan Gillean, Sgurr a'Bhasteir, Fionn Choire and Bruach na Frithe at sundown

Plate 135 Skye magic

The purpose of this book is not to give special publicity to any of the hotels in Skye, but the Sligachan Hotel is so well known to climbers and tourists that it merits some notice in these pages. Standing near the head of Loch Sligachan, it occupies one of the most desolate situations in this desolate island, with the rolling moors stretching away in all directions and frowned upon by Sgurr nan Gillean and the ever present Coolins. The hotel has been modernised in recent years, is almost luxuriously comfortable, and famed for its cuisine. Its rooms are especially attractive to the mountaineer because the walls are decorated with many lovely pictures painted by artists of note, whilst the fine prints of the Coolins taken by that well-known pioneer Lakeland photographer, Mr. A. P. Abraham, are a delight to everyone who sees them. A Post Office is attached to the hotel and buses give connections to all parts of Skye so that every guest, though he may imagine himself stranded away in the wilds, is in fact in easy touch with the outside world (137).

Those visitors who are interested in photography will find innumerable subjects at the very doors of the hotel. For instance, a small pool lies just beside the road near the bridge over the Sligachan River and on the rather infrequent calm days it provides an attractive foreground in which many beautiful scenes are mirrored (138 and 140). The most artistic canvas, however, is afforded by the vista to the south along Glen Sligachan where the enclosing hills frame the shapely Marsco, with the sweeping curves of the Sligachan River in the foreground; a scene painted by many famous artists, some of whose pictures of it adorn the lounge of the hotel (136 and Frontispiece). Those who like nature studies will not have to wander far afield because wild flowers in abundance carpet the boggy moorland, and the nodding heads of the white cotton-grass are conspicuous on the edges of the pools nearby (139). Sheep, too, amble about the adjacent sparse grasslands where they and their lambs make all sorts of attractive subjects in the spring; but if they can be captured with one of the mountain groups in the background, then the resulting

Plate 136 Marsco and Glen Sligachan with the river in spate

photograph is more interesting and is raised from the commonplace snap to the more artistic exhibition print (135).

Even if the ordinary wayfarer comes to Sligachan and has no special hobby to engage his attention, he will find plenty of exercise in the vicinity and have every opportunity of seeing some fine scenery without climbing the more difficult peaks. Let him take the track over the bridge down the eastern side of the river in Glen Sligachan. This will lead him to the desolate stretches of the valley and as he penetrates more deeply he will be surprised how far he has to walk before he passes the great bastions of Sgurr nan Gillean on his right (141). Here he will discover the two lonely lochans near the entrance to Harta Corrie; whilst these views are of undoubted grandeur, he still has to go a few miles further if he wishes to see the real splendour of Blaven, hidden round the corner of Ruadh Stac. One of the best viewpoints is at the ford where the Coruisk track crosses the burn and from here he will see the majestic flank of the mountain rising in one unbroken sweep of 3,000 feet (914 m), and on its left, the shattered crest of Clach Glas whose traverse is one of the tit-bits of the mountaineer (142).

If the pedestrian is so full of energy that he must set out to break records, let him attempt to beat the almost mythical time for the ascent of Glamaig. The best way to climb this conical peak is first to walk down the road to Loch Sligachan (143), and then to breast its north-west slopes, avoiding wherever possible the scree so as to make good time (144). If he reaches the summit in an hour he will not have done badly, and here he may linger on the soft mossy top and admire the comprehensive view which is one of the rewards of the ascent. Let him return by way of Beinn Dearg and so take in the whole of Lord Macdonald's Forest in one exhilarating walk. And if he still wants more to conquer in the day, let him include Marsco in the circuit, for he will then return to Sligachan and feel proud of his exploits!

The angler, too, will find plenty of sport near Sligachan, for the lochs are full of brown trout, and salmon lurk in the burns. Whilst he may ply his rod and line in solitude on any day of the week, let him beware, however, for it is said the fish here never bite on a Sunday!

Plate 137 The Sligachan Hotel

Plate 138 The Gooling mirrored in a small Shirachap Ichhar

Plate 139 Cotton grass on the boggy moorland

Plate 140 Masses by rocks; morning light

Plate 141 Sgurr nan Gillean from Glen Sligachan

Plate 142 Clach Glas and Blaven from Strath Craithgeach.

Plate 143 An afternoon in May by Loch Sligachan

Broadford, on the shores of one of the most beautiful bays in Skye, is a splendid holiday centre for those who visit the island with a car (145). It possesses some fine hotels as well as every other type of accommodation and has interesting little shops—a feature missing from many of the remote places. Whilst it is too far away from the Coolins to appeal to the mountaineer, there are plenty of stiff walks on the Red Hills nearby; but the great charm of the village is that it is so near Loch Slapin and Elgol. These, however, are too far distant for a return walk in a day but are easily visited by car. To travellers who have a taste for fine mountain scenery this excursion is one of the most repaying on the Misty Isle.

Leave Broadford by a narrow road which at first follows a south-westerly course, with Beinn na Caillich rising across the moors on your right. After many twists and turns you come to the reedy Loch Cill Chriosd where the road skirts its southern shore, and as you leave it behind you notice the frowning summit of Blaven peeping over the lower slopes of Beinn Dearg Bheag. This is the first sight you get of this mighty mountain, and as you advance along the road your eye will be continually drawn to it as the whole of this chain of hills is unfolded, bit by bit, until as you approach Kilbride they stand before you in all their glory. Blaven rises at the southern end of the range and the skyline to the right of it passes over the serrated crest of Clach Glas, and then over Gars-bheinn with the lesser Sgurr nan Each in front of it. Afterwards it dips considerably before rising again to Belig and finally encompasses Glas Bheinn Mhor (146).

At Kilbride you are still four miles (6·76 km) away from Blaven. As you approach it through Torrin and then drop down to the shore of Loch Slapin, its majesty will overwhelm you and you will probably agree with many artists who have painted it, that together with its satellites it forms one of the most magnificent mountain scenes in the country (147).

The road skirts the shore of the loch with enchanting views at every bend, but when you turn south at its head, do not forget to look back occasionally at the revealing views of the Red Hills. On the left you will see the wedge-shaped peak of Beinn na Cro, frowning upon the higher reaches of the loch and facing the long summit ridge of Glas Bheinn Mhor to the west across the verdant stretches of Strath, which provides a short cut for pedestrians from Loch Ainort (148). To the right you will espy the cottages of Torrin standing cheek by jowl with Beinn na Caillich (149).

The rough mountain road rises steeply to Keppoch and then falls to the houses of Kirkibost, where, if you are so minded, you may get out of your car and walk across the moor to ascend the long escarpment of Blaven, whose summit ridge affords magnificent views of both Coolins and sea. If, however, you continue along the road you will skirt the slopes of Ben Meabost and from its crest look across the sea to the Point of Sleat on the left, beyond which are spread out across the ocean the islands of Eigg, Rhum and Canna not far away to the south-west. You then begin the descent to Elgol and, on rounding the slopes of the diminutive Ben Cleat, the great peaks of the Coolins appear one by one, first Gars-bheinn, and then the rest of them, until, when you finally reach the last house of this hamlet the graceful lines of Sgurr nan Gillean rise behind Sgurr na Stri on the right, their slopes enclosing Loch Scavaig whose waves beat upon the rocky shore at your feet.

This view is one of the wonders of Skye and its magic appeals to everyone who is lucky enough to see it. If you are a mountaineer and familiar with the Coolins, you can pick out all the peaks except those hidden by the great ridge of the Dubhs, and will doubtless recall the many happy days you have spent climbing them. If you are a tourist who loves the mountain landscape, you too will here find much to please, for nowhere else in Britain will you see such an array of shapely hills all rising directly from the sea. If you observe this magnificent panorama under favourable conditions, when the subtle colouring of the hills and the delicate hues of the sky combine with the azure reaches of Loch Scavaig to make such a lovely picture, it will live for ever in your memory (150).

Plate 145 Looking to the mainland peaks from Broadford

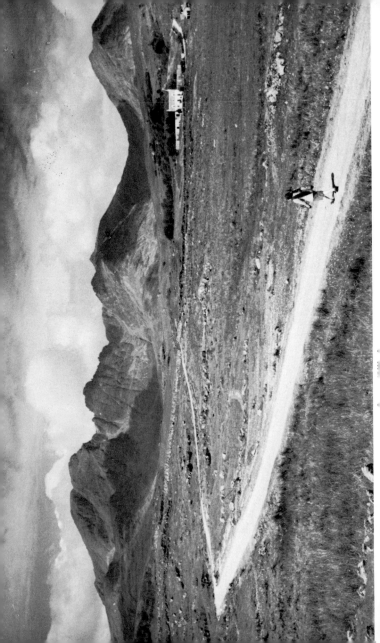

Plate 147 Blaven, Clach Glas and Sgurr nan Each from Loch Slapin

Plate 148 Glas Bheinn Mhor and Beinn na Cro

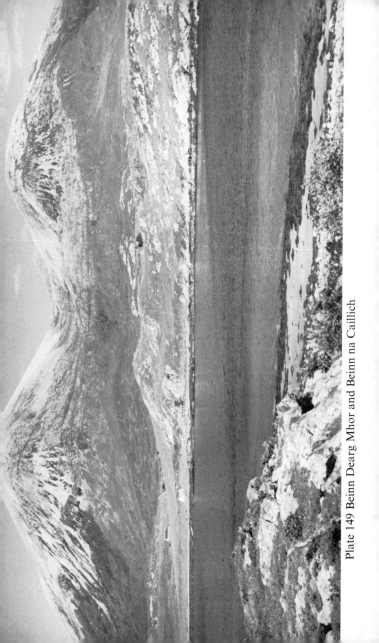

Plate 149 Beinn Dearg Mhor and Beinn na Caillich

Plate 150 The Coolins from Elgol

Plate 151 I bid farewell to the magic hills of Skye

I happen to be one of the mountaineers cited at the end of the last monograph and I came to Elgol on a perfect day in June to bid farewell to this lovely isle. I was accompanied by two friends with a similar affection for this country, and in wandering down the green slopes leading to the shore of Loch Scavaig we trod a carpet of luscious grass, sprinkled with several varieties of wild orchids, precious little flowers which I had not seen before in Skye. In due course we reached the basaltic strata which edges the restless sea, and sat down there quietly to contemplate the superb panorama spread out before us.

White clouds floated serenely overhead while I passed in review my many delightful experiences on this wonderful island. The Coolins naturally occupied my first thoughts in this soliloquy because I could see their peaks so clearly against the sky, and had I not climbed them all, sometimes with the Good Companions, and sometimes in solitary state? Then there were those marvellous days on the Storr and Quiraing whose bizarre rock architecture had been more spectacular than anything else I had seen in our homeland. But even these were only a few of the brilliant facets of this flashing jewel whose pageant of beauty had captivated me so completely during the last few weeks.

The next morning the metamorphosis of the scene was complete, for during the night the Gods had decreed a return of the bad weather, and when I left the island the rain poured down in torrents to blot out its wild landscape. It is strange, in this short life, how we all quickly forget the unpleasant experiences and remember only the happy ones, and for me, Skye will be no exception to this rule. Although I have seen it in a variety of moods, I shall always think of it as I have portrayed it in this book, and I hope those who are tempted to follow in my footsteps will receive an equally glorious impression of this Masterpiece of Nature.

The unerring eye of my camera may have missed some of its lovely scenes, and my descriptions of its enchantment may convey only a modicum of its real charm, but you, dear reader, may have been there, and already come under its magic spell. If, however, you are a mountaineer, I know the peaks of the Coolins will call to you again and again until you finally climb the hills of Eternity.

This book, then, should conjure up cherished memories of the happy days you have spent on the Misty Isle, but if you are not of the Elect, you may still turn its pages and perhaps be induced to go there and steep yourself in its magic too.

Photographers who have studied the plates in this book will know that Skye offers unlimited opportunities to all those who have an eye for a picture. A large proportion of the photographs were taken from places easily accessible to any surefooted pedestrian, but those who have read the text will understand that casual walkers interested in this hobby cannot wander about at will on the Coolins as they can on the hills of Lakeland, Snowdonia and much of the Highlands. If, therefore, they wish to click their shutters on the splintered peaks of the Main Ridge, they should go to either Glen Brittle or Sligachan and ask one of the climbers there to guide them up to some of the more easily attained tops, otherwise they may find themselves in alarming situations and experience the indignity of having to be rescued and brought back to safety! Those, however, who are satisfied to take the *Easy Ways for the Walker* outlined in these pages need have no qualms about getting back home and, on these routes, they will have ample opportunities of toying with their cameras.

The weather in Skye has proved disappointing to many photographers and especially to those who have been unable to spend long vacations on the island. Sometimes I had to wait for days on end before I obtained suitable lighting and even then conditions were not as perfect as I could have wished. As it was, I did the best I could in the circumstances, and since I had booked no definite accommodation in advance, I was largely at the mercy of hotel proprietors, who fortunately appreciated my difficulties and were kind enough to reserve my rooms until I was ready to move on. This is more easily arranged early in the season and if I had made this journey later in the year, it is doubtful whether I should have been permitted to wait so long for the light and I then could not have secured many of the camera studies reproduced in these pages.

When planning this tour I had included only one other excursion than those which now appear in this book. I had hoped to sail round the magnificent coast of Loch Bracadale from MacLeod's Maidens to Talisker Bay, because it provides some of the finest seascapes in Skye. When the perfect day dawned, as I thought, I was bitterly disappointed to find the owner of the only available boat unwilling to risk his craft on the rough sea.

In view of these trials and tribulations the following notes on the various monographs may be helpful to those who wish to follow in my footsteps.

PORTREE. There are not so many subjects here as one might imagine but those who are lucky enough to be in the town on a calm day will secure some pleasing shots of the houses round the harbour reflected in the little bay. If they have plenty of time to walk over Ben Tianavaig and to return along the sea edge below it, they will discover an abundance of fine foregrounds to show off the harbour and cliffs to the north of it.

THE ROAD TO STAFFIN. This twenty-mile (34 km) journey gave me all the opportunities I wanted, but I should have preferred a clearer atmosphere for the shot of Staffin Bay because the hills of the mainland would then have been more easily seen in the background. There are many attractive crofters' cottages near the road but the problem is to photograph them showing their situation with the hills in the background. There is only one viewpoint on the cliffs for the shot of the Kilt Rock, and of course every visitor has taken the photograph reproduced herein. I thought a wide-angle lens might be an advantage but on looking through the viewfinder I found it wasn't and did not use it. Those who could arrange to sail up the coast of Trotternish would probably obtain some fine pictures of its wonderful seaboard with the striking ridge in the background.

THE STORR. I have portrayed all that is of interest in this bizarre collection of rocks but some of the pictures would have been better with a fine sky.

LEAC na'FIONN. I was lucky on this climb for conditions were perfect. I did try to photograph its eastern precipice from below but the results were nothing like so good as those reproduced in these pages. The only fine shot I missed was of the group as a whole seen from the cliff face below Quiraing, but on looking round for a suitable foreground, which, by the way, is extremely

Plate 152 Contact print with plate numbers

difficult to find, I missed the light which went off the subject in
the interval. I subsequently considered it from the vicinity of the
Table when the light was favourable but I found the viewpoint
was too high to reveal its most striking elevation.

QUIRAING. The usual picture one sees of this superlative
subject is taken from the south side of the sharp bend in the
Staffin-Uig road which appears in the foreground. To say the
best of it, is that it is hackneyed, for it gives no idea of the
grandeur of this marvellous scene. I could not have done better
in any circumstances and am sure the plates accompanying this
monograph will be a revelation.

DUNTULM. The ruins of this castle and its fine position will
appeal to all photographers, but strangely enough it is generally
taken from the west with the result that its real situation is not
disclosed. I studied it from all angles and am satisfied with plate
50.

GLEN BRITTLE. The difficulty here is to convey a correct
impression of its fine location at the foot of the Coolins and I
hope I have succeeded. I had ample opportunities of exploring
the adjacent ground in favourable lighting, but perhaps I might
have done better by taking a telephoto shot of it from one of the
low hills on the west side of the valley.

THE WESTERN CORRIES. I spent much time in trying to discover
a revealing viewpoint for Coire Lagan, not only in the corrie
itself, but also on the precipitous southern façade of Sgurr Dearg.
The proximity of this vast basin, however, while appealing
strongly to the eye, is too immense for the camera and I had to

be satisfied with plate 58. Actually this was taken too late in the day to do the scene full justice and two hours earlier would have afforded better side lighting which would have given greater contrasts in the crags of both Alasdair and Sgumain. I was more fortunate in Coir'a'Ghrunnda and secured several revealing shots but scarcity of space permits the inclusion of only two of them. The vastness of both Coire na Banachdich and Coire a'Ghreadaidh make them difficult to photograph effectively and I failed in the latter after spending a whole afternoon waiting for the light. It is highly probable they would yield the best results from the hills on the other side of Glen Brittle. I went to Coire na Creiche with A. S. Taylor, one of the Good Companions and himself a keen photographer. Unhappily the light was weak but some years later I secured plate 62, from the far side of Glen Brittle, which reveals the whole Corrie to perfection.

RUDH' AN DUNAIN. The only disappointing feature about this walk was the persistent cloud cap on the Coolins which prevented me taking telephoto shots of Coire Lagan and Coir'a'Ghrunnda from the moorland. Otherwise the light was perfect for the seascapes which speak for themselves. There is a moot point which deserves mention in connection with the possible viewpoints for plate 64. The lie of the land is such that this scene may be photographed from a series of different heights above the sea, and it is a question whether the headland looks better against the sky, or as I have shown it revealing the ocean on its far side. I have seen several prints of this subject by well-known photographers and they appear to be undecided as to the best of these coigns of vantage, but in most cases they have failed to include any rocks in the foreground, which to my mind is a mistake.

LOCH CORUISK. This magnificent subject proved to be my Waterloo, for on each of my three visits I was defeated by the weather. Apart from the sombre grandeur of the loch itself, the head of Loch Scavaig affords many lovely shots for the camera. I am, however, convinced that the best viewpoint for the former is the summit of Sgurr na Stri and had my long stay at Sligachan been graced by better weather I should have made a fourth attempt to reach this distant hill top under more favourable conditions.

WATERSTEIN HEAD. I have been aware of this subject for at least three decades, but poor approach roads delayed my first visit. In the meantime, however, the road to Glendale was improved and only then did I drive to its terminus, high above the sea. Afternoon is the best time for visiting photographers, as the sun has then passed its zenith and so illuminates the western facing cliffs; after 3 p.m. the lighting is perfect on a favourable day. Although I have since been there on several occasions I have never enjoyed perfect lighting for the Headland, whose great height can only be appreciated if a boat happens to be near its base.

SGURR ALASDAIR. I did better on this dominating peak than I had expected, but this was due to the changing conditions while I happened to be there. Like many other parts of the Coolins, this mountain demands the use of a wide angle lens and those who do not possess one will miss many of its possibilities.

SRON NA CICHE. This great face of rock requires late evening lighting for its effective portrayal together with some figures in the foreground, if the immensity of its scale is to be appreciated. The lie of the land on the north side of Coire Lagan does not help in the solution of this problem and plate 57 was the best I could do. The Cioch is a spectacular subject which has been hackneyed by all mountain photographers and the Good Companions defied me to make something more of it than my predecessors. Whether I have succeeded is for them to judge, but those who do not know it should remember that the light in the afternoon is straight into the lens of the camera, which, coupled with the restricted viewpoint, makes its portrayal far from easy. Plates 83 and 84 are, I think, a new angle on this climb, at least I have not seen them before.

THE MAIN COOLINS RIDGE FROM GARS-BHEINN TO SGURR DEARG. The mountain scene revealed from the Main Ridge of the Coolins provided such an endless variety of striking and beautiful photographs that I could easily have devoted a whole book to it. I decided, however, that this volume would have a wider appeal if it included the general characteristics of Skye as well as pictures of specific interest to climbers, and in consequence I had severely to cut down the plates covering this particular aspect of the island. In doing so I was faced by several peculiar problems of selection, because my first consideration was to give mountaineers a comprehensive idea of the Main Ridge and at the same time to choose pictorial subjects which would effectively convey its topography. As a case in point I need only mention the Thearlaich-Dubh Gap. This spectacular *mauvais pas* is usually photographed either from the crest of its short side to show the detail of its long side, or else from the base of the Gap looking out. But neither of these viewpoints give an adequate idea of its situation or inaccessibility and the only photograph I have seen which attempted to convey this impression was taken by Mr. G. Starkey. After studying this subject from all angles I took only four photographs of it: one from immediately above the long side of the Gap which showed a part of the short side with the Dubhs in the background; another from an awkward stance on the precipitous eastern face of Alasdair which gave a slightly different angle to the same view; and two from different heights on the eastern face of Sgumain. On subsequently examining the four prints I had no hesitation in selecting plate 89 which was taken from the lower of the last two viewpoints because it not only reveals the situation and elevation of the Gap, but is also the most pictorial rendering of it.

The southern section of the Main Ridge as far as Sgurr Thearlaich affords unlimited scope to the mountain photographer, but the short stretch from here to Sgurr Dearg presents an almost insoluble problem because the few effective viewpoints are so restricted. I thought Sgurr Alasdair might be the best coign of vantage for it, but I did not much care for the pictures I took there and eventually came to the conclusion that those I had taken from Sgumain would be the best.

SGURRS DEARG AND BANACHDICH. The topography of the main and lateral ridges of these two mountains allows plenty of freedom of movement with a consequent variety of viewpoints and subjects. Although I climbed them both twice, and waited on the summit of Sgurr Dearg on one occasion for two hours, I had not more than ten minutes of sunshine in which to take the photographs of it, which illustrate this monograph. Those who are familiar with this terrain will know I had to move about with considerable alacrity to secure them and this involved running along the whole ridge to obtain plates 97 and 95. I only arrived there just in time because within thirty seconds of clicking the shutter the gap in the clouds had closed, never to re-open again that afternoon. Those readers who still doubt the superiority of the modern miniature camera as the ideal instrument for the mountain photographer may care to speculate on the results they would have obtained with a more cumbersome instrument in these circumstances.

Plate 96 of the Inaccessible Pinnacle is much hackneyed and of course gives a completely misleading impression of this strange feature of Sgurr Dearg: by including Plates 93 and 94 I have, however, exploded this myth! I scrambled down to An Stac and photographed its obverse aspect with two of the Good Companions climbing its exposed crest, but as the light was bad it did not merit inclusion herein.

The most spectacular scene from this mountain is undoubtably that of Alasdair and its satellites as portrayed in Plate 95. It is usually photographed from a lower point on the lateral ridge where the foreground is not so good, but this viewpoint has one advantage in that Sgurr Mhic Coinnich and the gap in the ridge below it are then silhouetted against the sky instead of being confused by the Dubhs in the background.

THE TRAVERSE OF SGURR A'GHREADAIDH. While no one would choose a cloudless sky and a hazy atmosphere as the ideal conditions for this traverse, I suppose I should not complain, but consider myself fortunate in being permitted to photograph this spectacular part of the Main Ridge from end to end without irritating delays waiting for the light. The monotony of this desolate landscape will, however, be apparent, but better conditions with the accompanying clouds and their shadows would have lent variety by softening much of its barrenness. The vista of Loch Coruisk is enchanting throughout this climb but its attractiveness is largely due to the colour contrasts between the greens of Coir-uisg, the purple blacks of the gabbro hills, and the deep blues of both loch and sea. A monochrome therefore loses much of this beauty and a cloudless sky eliminates all the lovely glitter usually reflected by water.

THE MAIN RIDGE TO BRUACH NA FRITHE. Considering the poor conditions I was very pleased with the results I obtained here. I should have liked to have included some closer shots of Bidein Druim nan Ramh and if I had been more fortunate with the weather at Sligachan, I had intended to photograph the three peaks of this group from the lateral ridge of Sgurr an Fheadain, because by afternoon light they are then revealed in their true form and elevation. The view of the twisting Main Ridge from Bruach na Frithe is often photographed and requires more brilliant lighting than I experienced. If it is taken about 7 p.m. B.S.T., the lights and shadows then reveal its topography perfectly and it makes a fine dramatic picture.

SGURR NAN GILLEAN AND SGURR A'BHASTEIR. All those who have studied the plates accompanying this monograph will have seen that these northern outposts of the Coolins make superb subjects for the camera, but it was only by a determined and prolonged attack upon them that I succeeded in my quest. During the three weeks in Sligachan I photographed Sgurr nan Gillean in a diverse variety of moods and I chose Plate 120 because it clearly discloses all the topographical features of this fine peak from the north. The only improvement I could have wished would have been in the lighting of the Pinnacle Ridge: Plate 130 was taken at 1 p.m. B.S.T., and 131, five hours later, whereas the ideal time would have been at 4 p.m. B.S.T. when the rays of the sun would have been at the correct angle across the Pinnacles to reveal every detail of their texture.

GLEN SLIGACHAN AND GLAMAIG. This series of studies gives an adequate impression of all that is to be seen here and I do not think I could have done better. I secured some attractive shots of the burns in spate and of the many lochans in the vicinity, but space would not permit of their inclusion in this book. Surprising though it may seem, Glamaig makes a good subject and I took a whole series of it one afternoon when returning down the path from the Bealach a'Mhaim. Once the Allt Dearg Cottage has been reached, its proximity demands the use of a wide angle lens, and although it is usually taken, showing Loch Sligachan on its left, I preferred Plate 144 because it includes a group of trees— rare subjects of foreground interest in this barren landscape.

BROADFORD TO ELGOL. The camera studies accompanying this monograph speak for themselves, but photographers who wish to emulate this series should remember that the light goes off the eastern face of Blaven at noontide. The one great nuisance here is the line of telegraph poles which run along the side of Loch Slapin, and although a herd of Highland cattle was grazing near the shore, it was impossible to get far enough away to use them in their proper perspective as foreground interest without the poles coming into the frame. Elgol affords a variety of foregrounds both high and low, and the rocky shore of Loch Scavaig is sufficiently broken to offer a wide enough choice to please the most fastidious camera artist.

FOOTNOTE. Climbers and mountain photographers have often posed this question—'How many shots do you have to take of any given subject to secure a satisfactory picture for inclusion in your books?' When I reply 'One only,' most of them seem incredulous, and so in order to convince them I have reproduced at the head of these notes a Contact Print of a strip of negatives, all of which appear in these pages!

Figures refer to plate numbers

Figures refer to page numbers.
Figures in bold refer to pages where monographs of the relevant items begin.